RELAXING
Stress Relief Coloring Book

Vol. 1

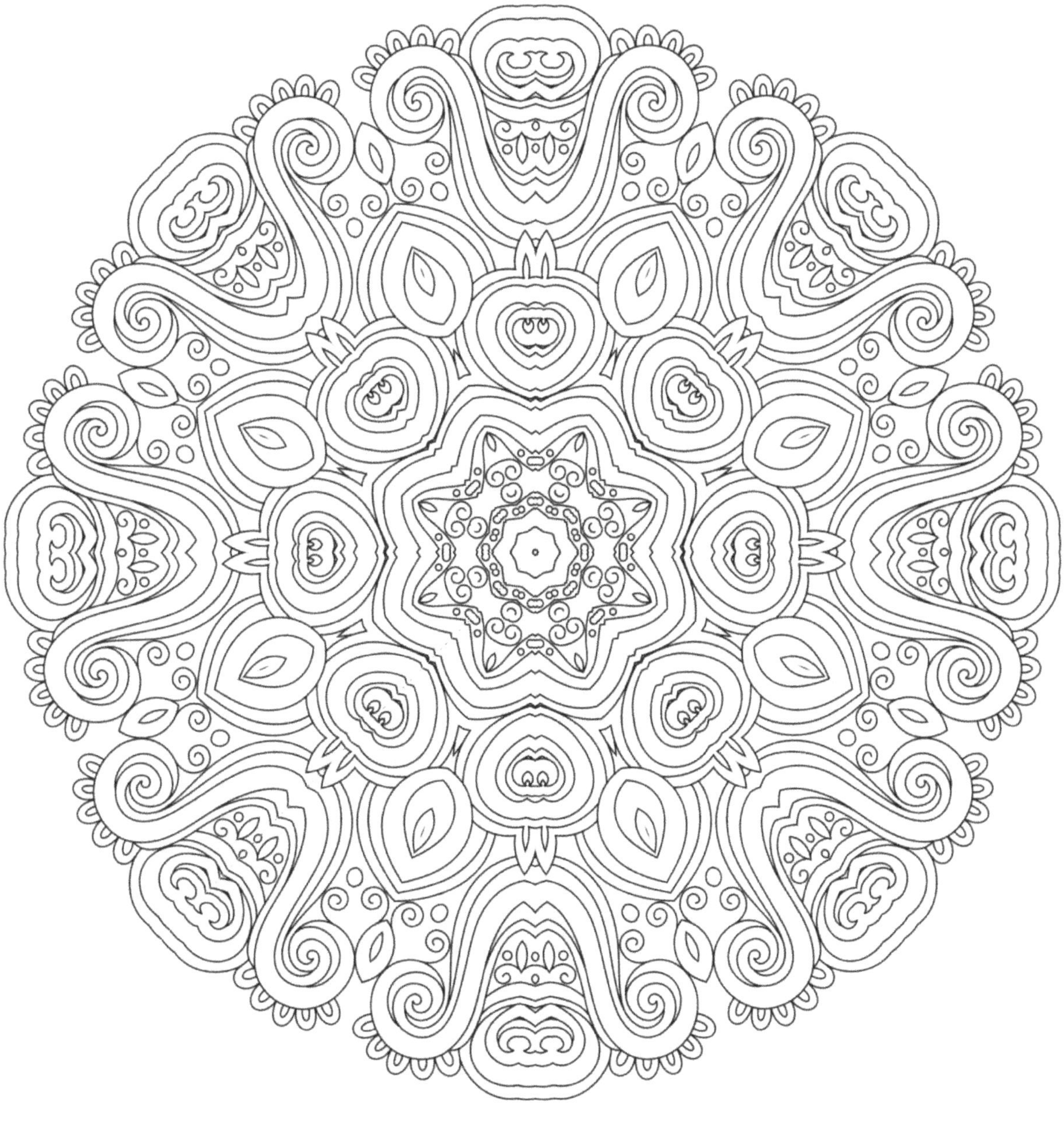

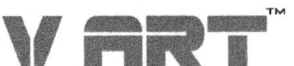

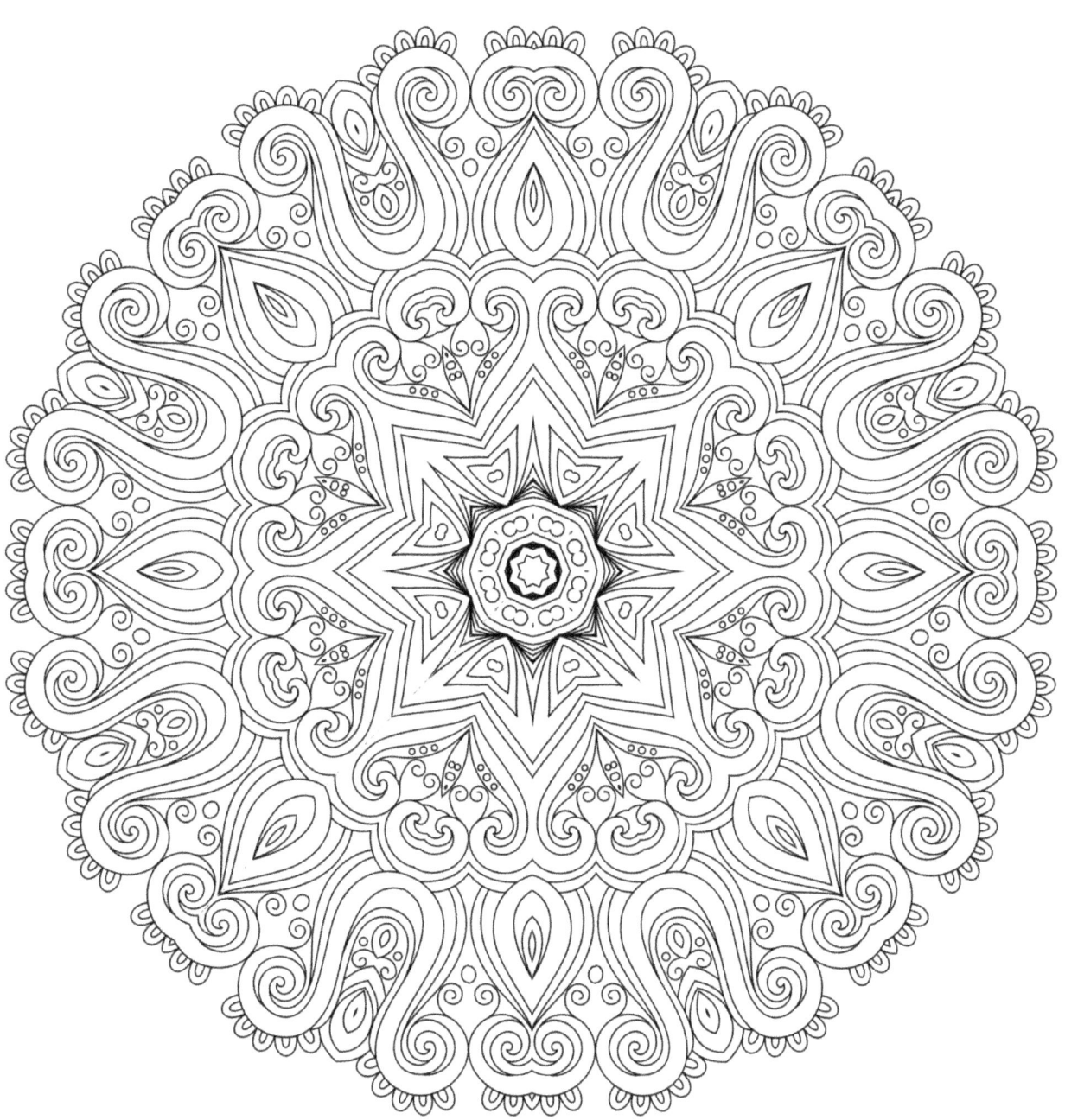

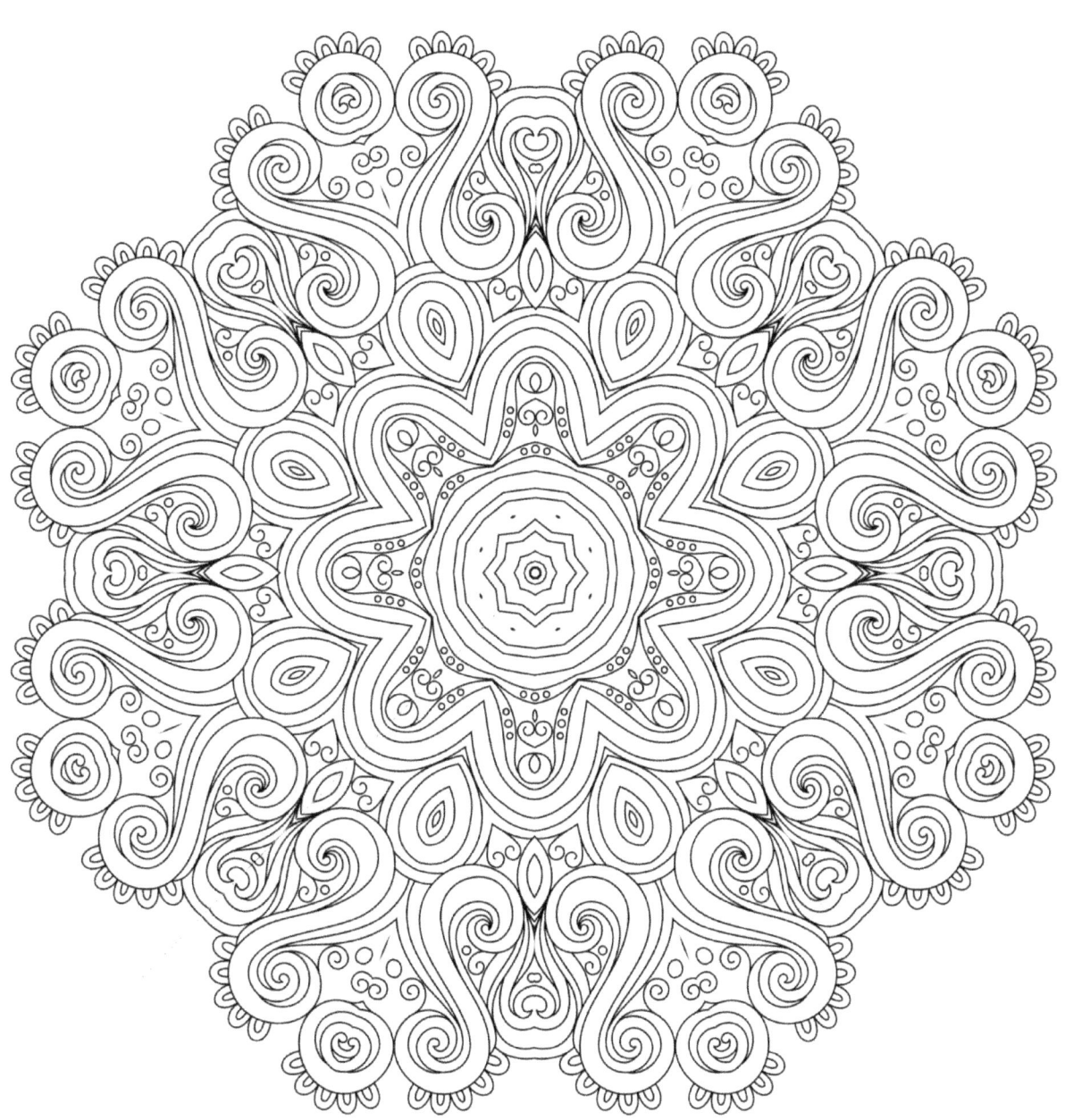

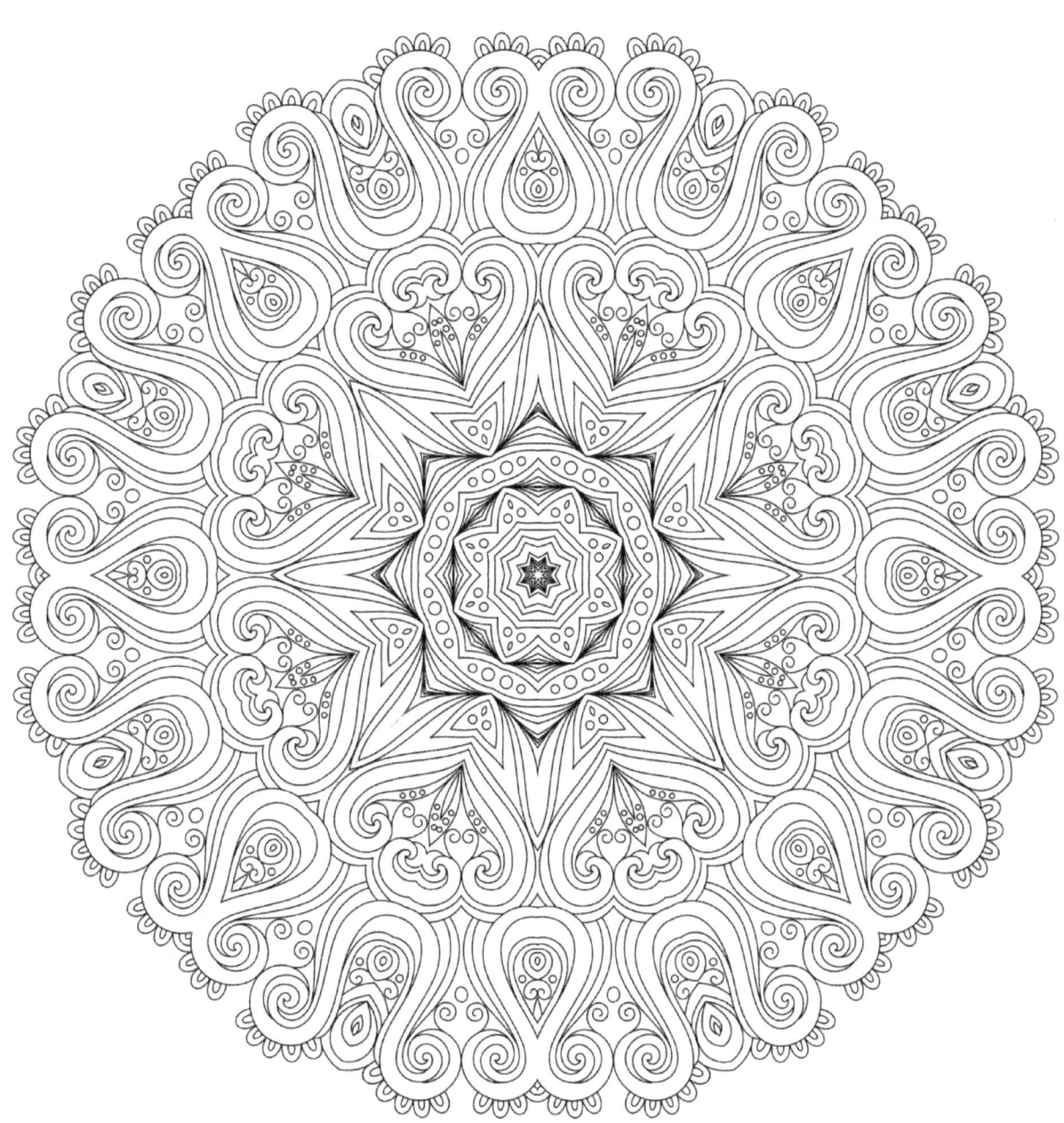

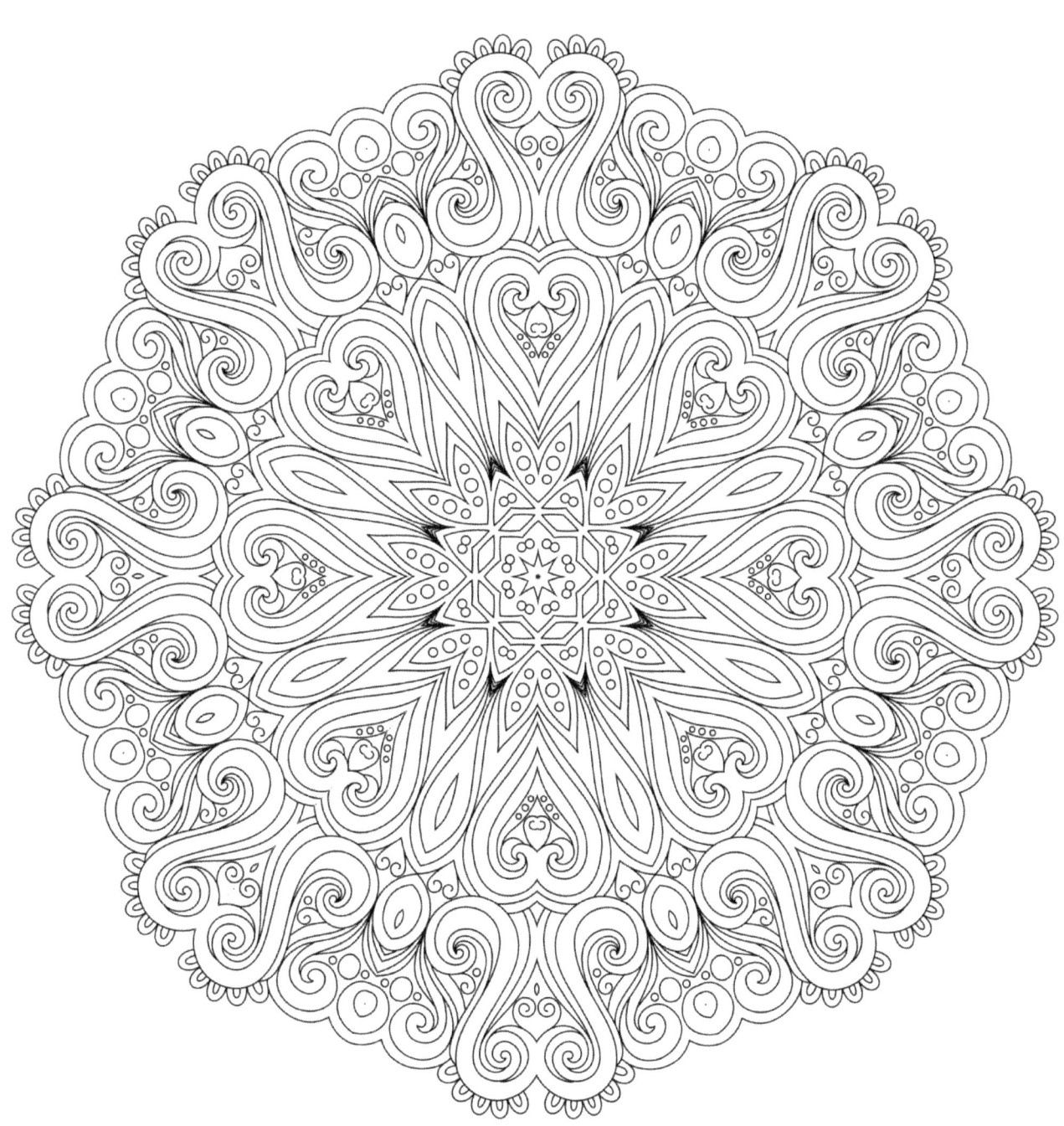

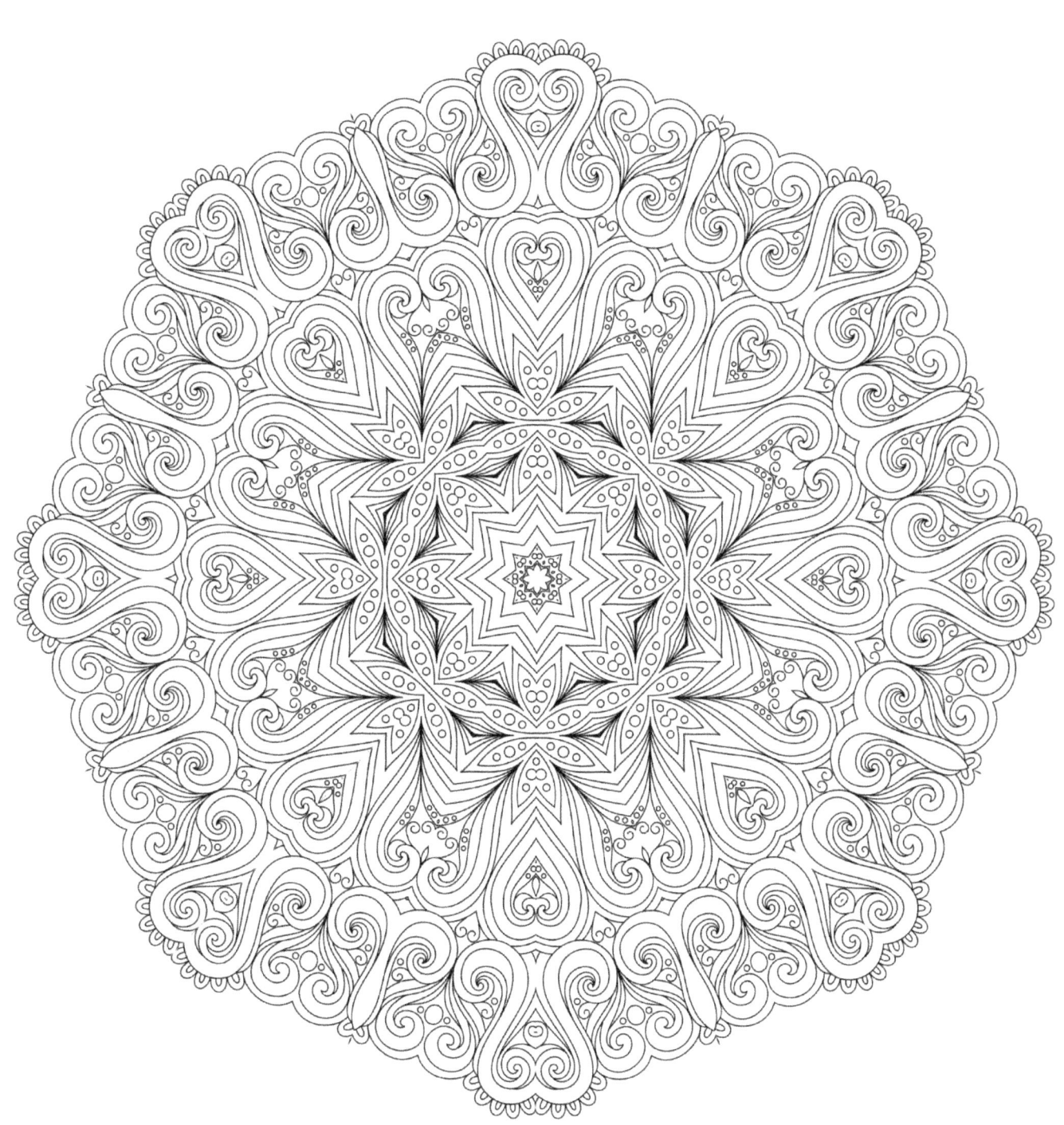

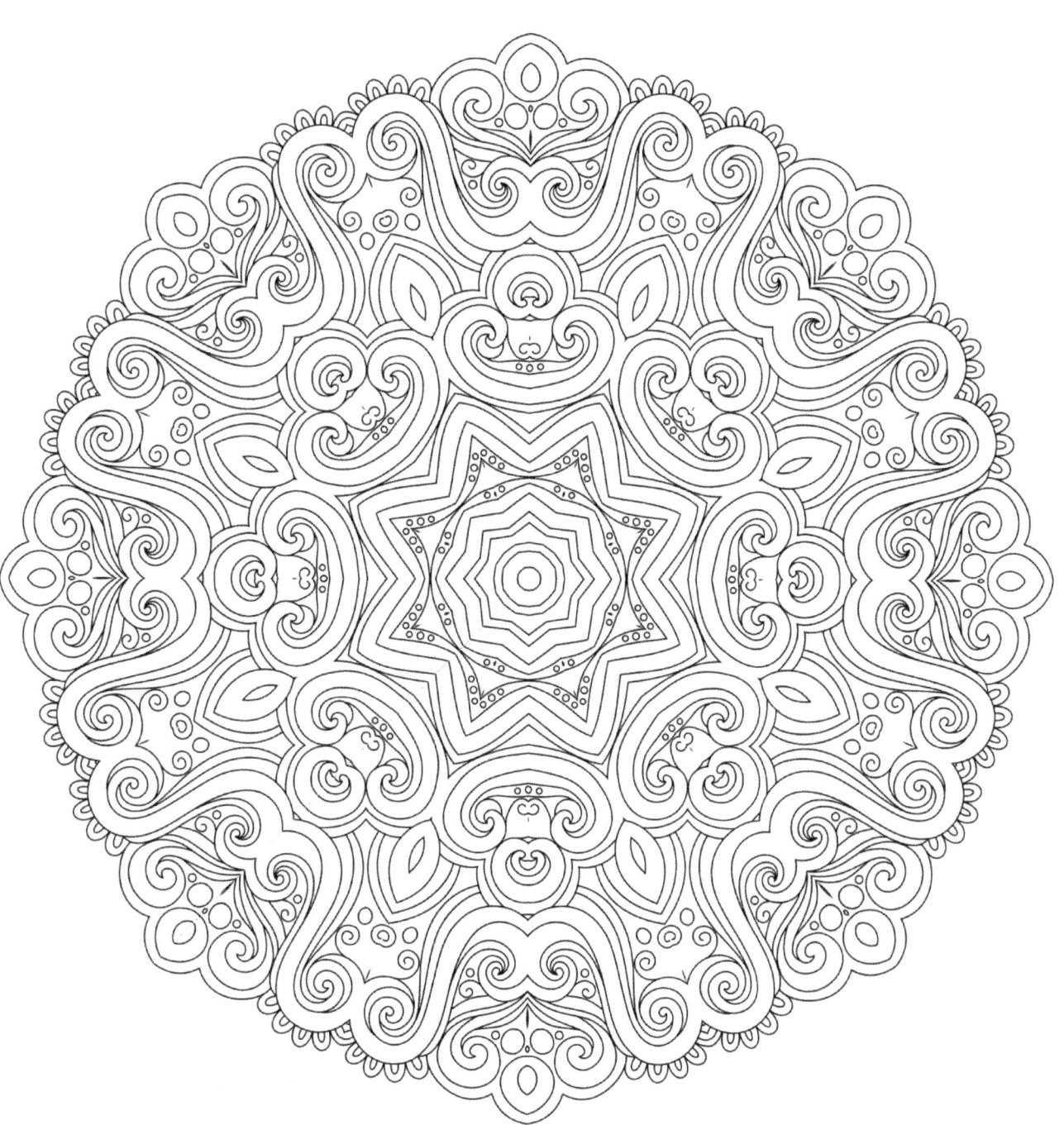

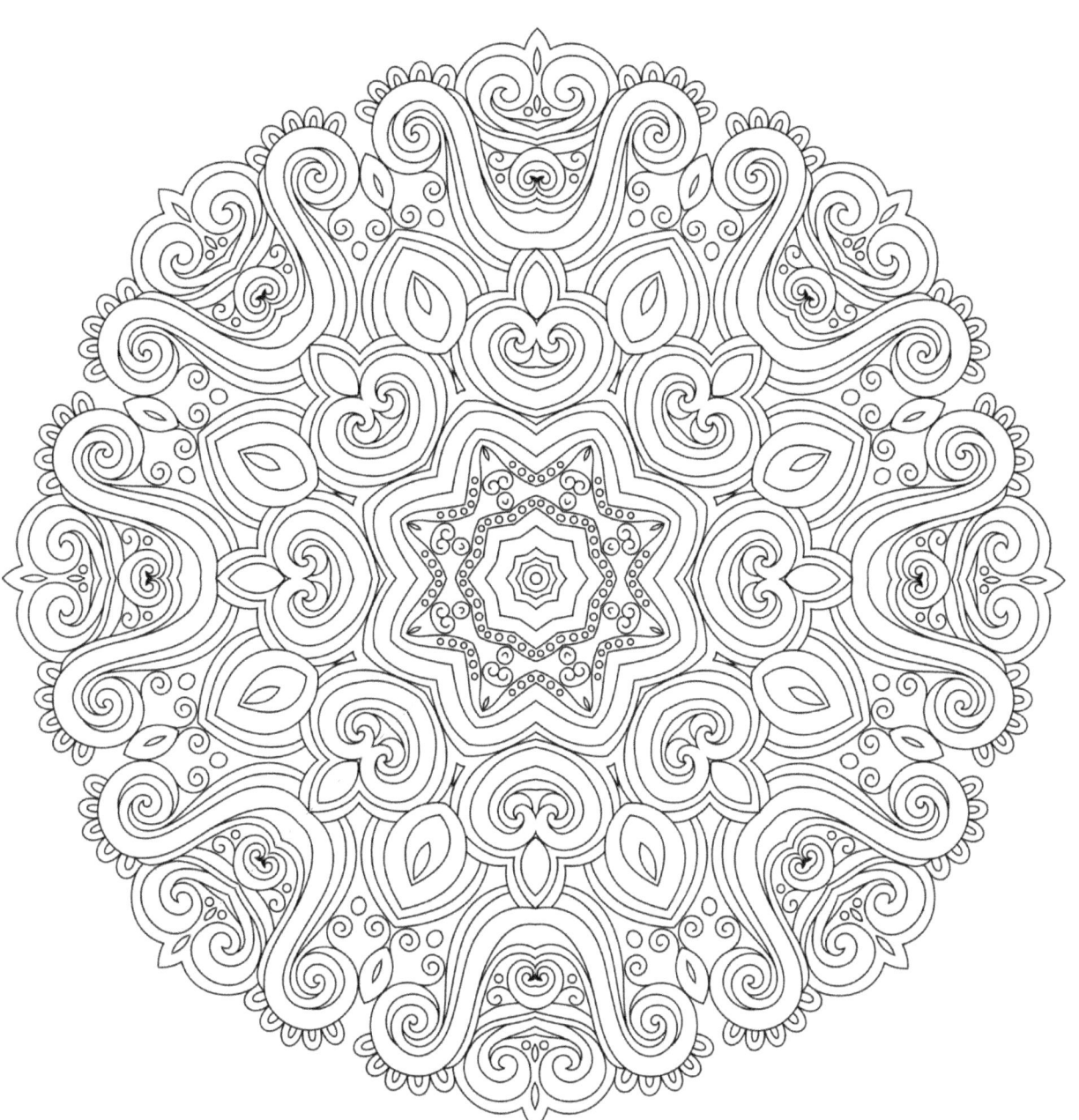

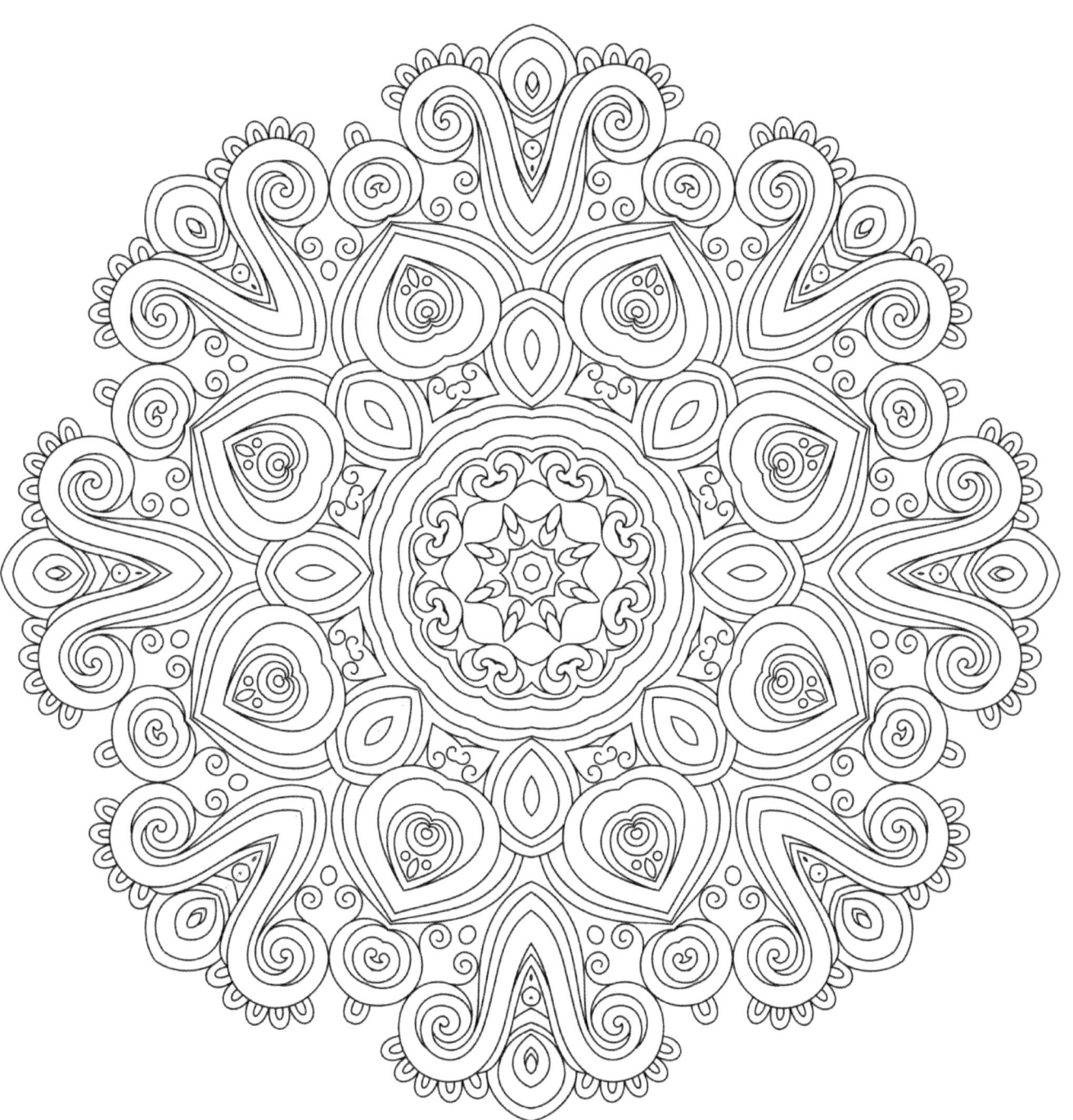

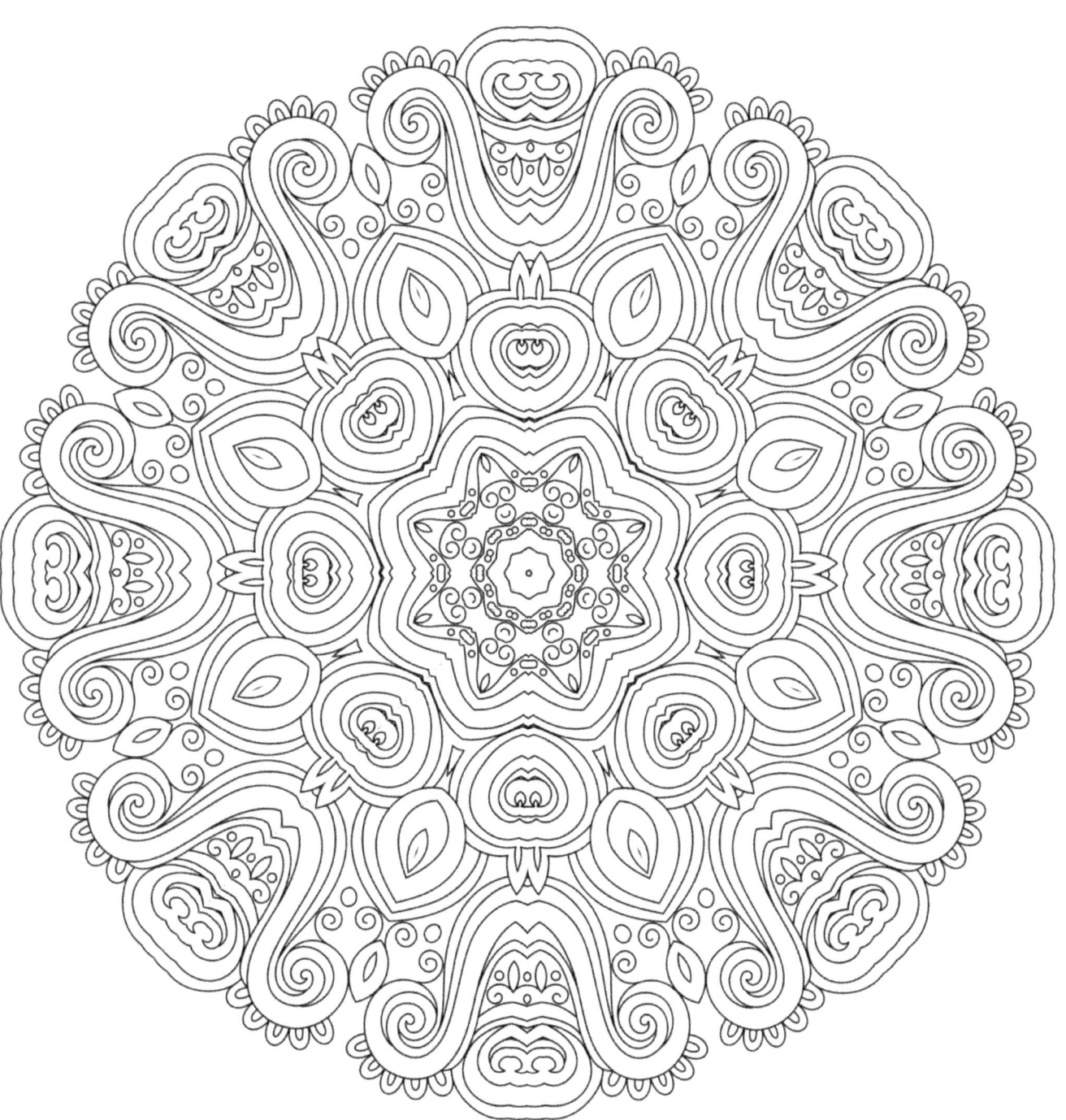

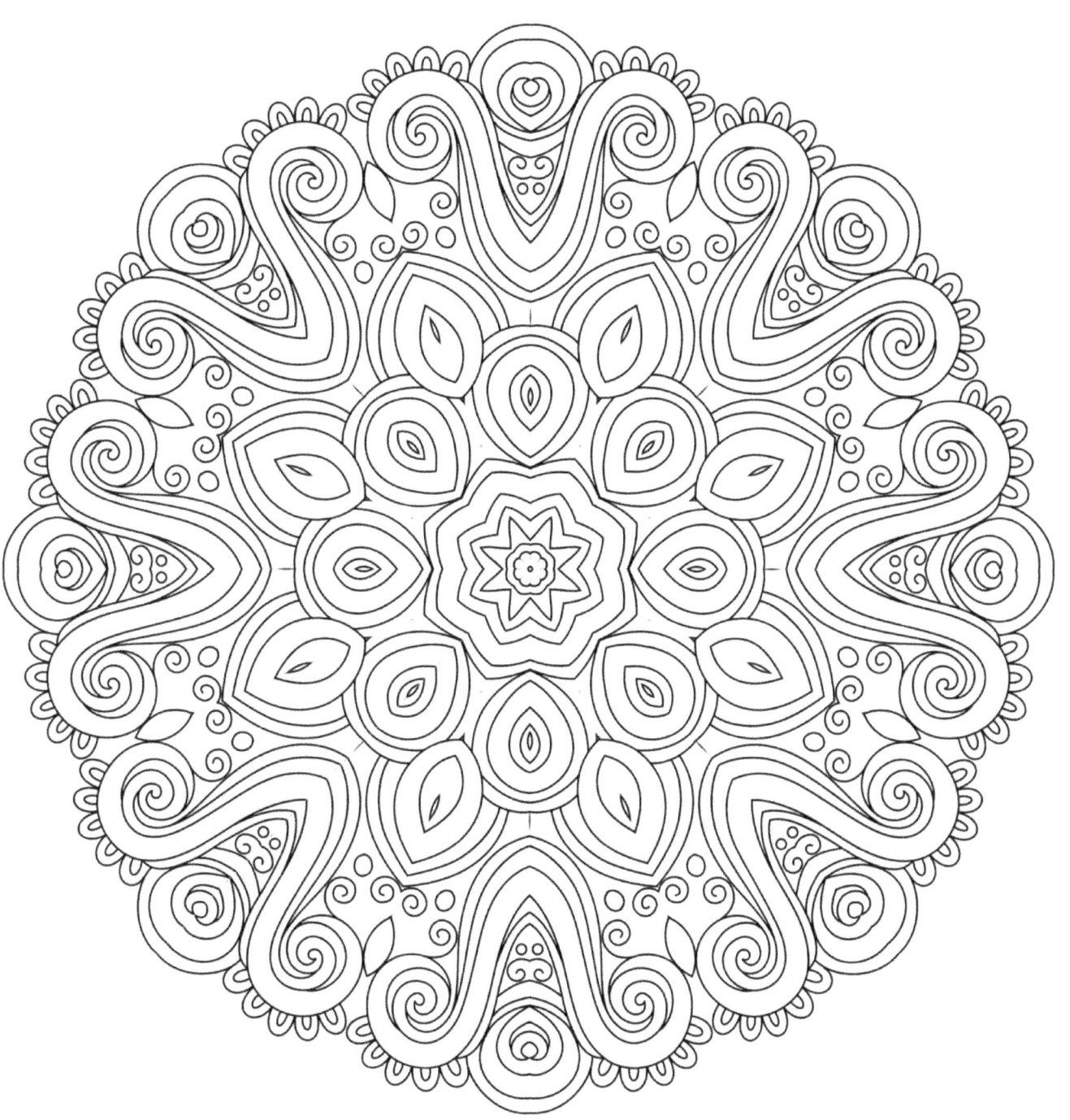

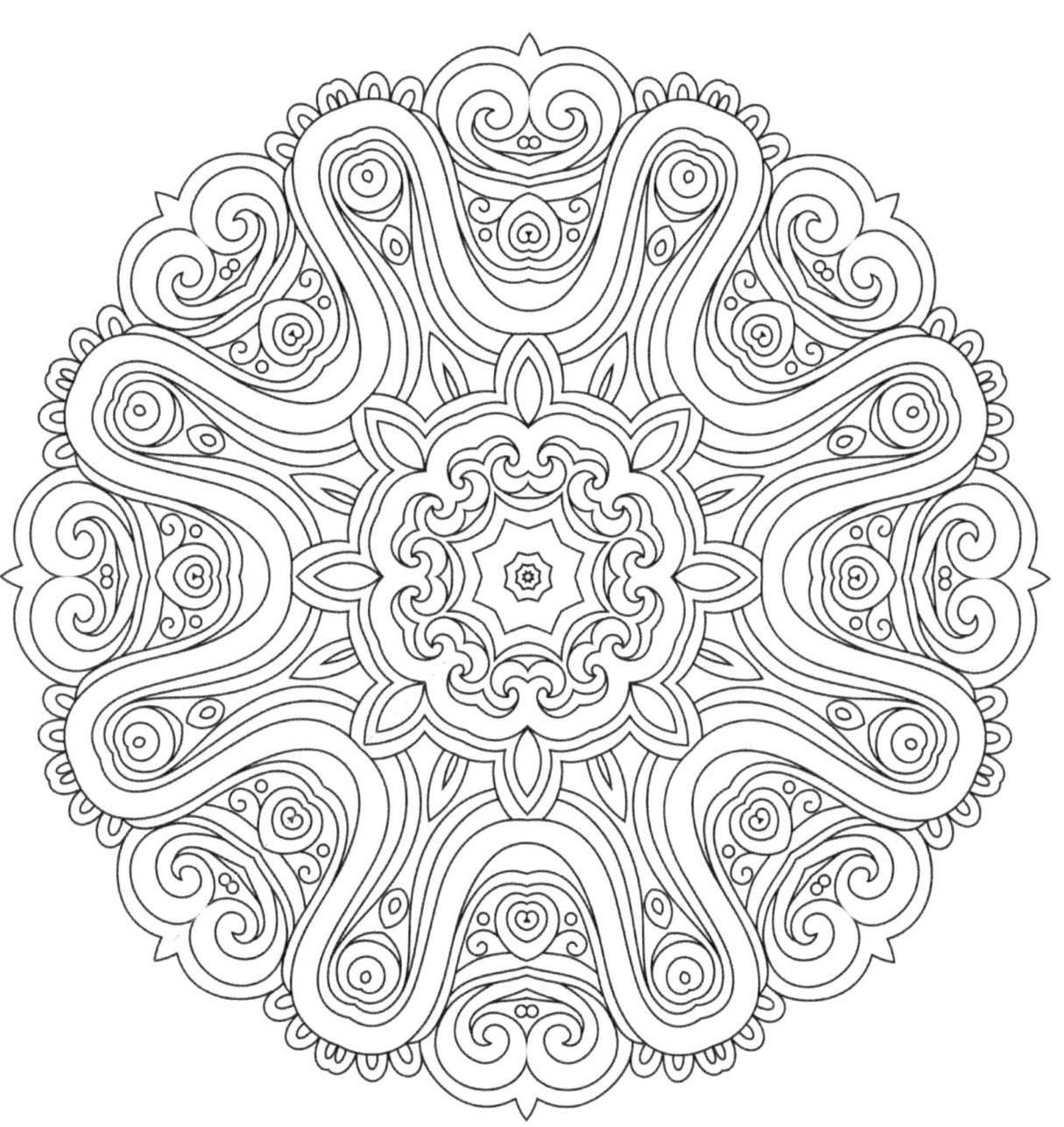

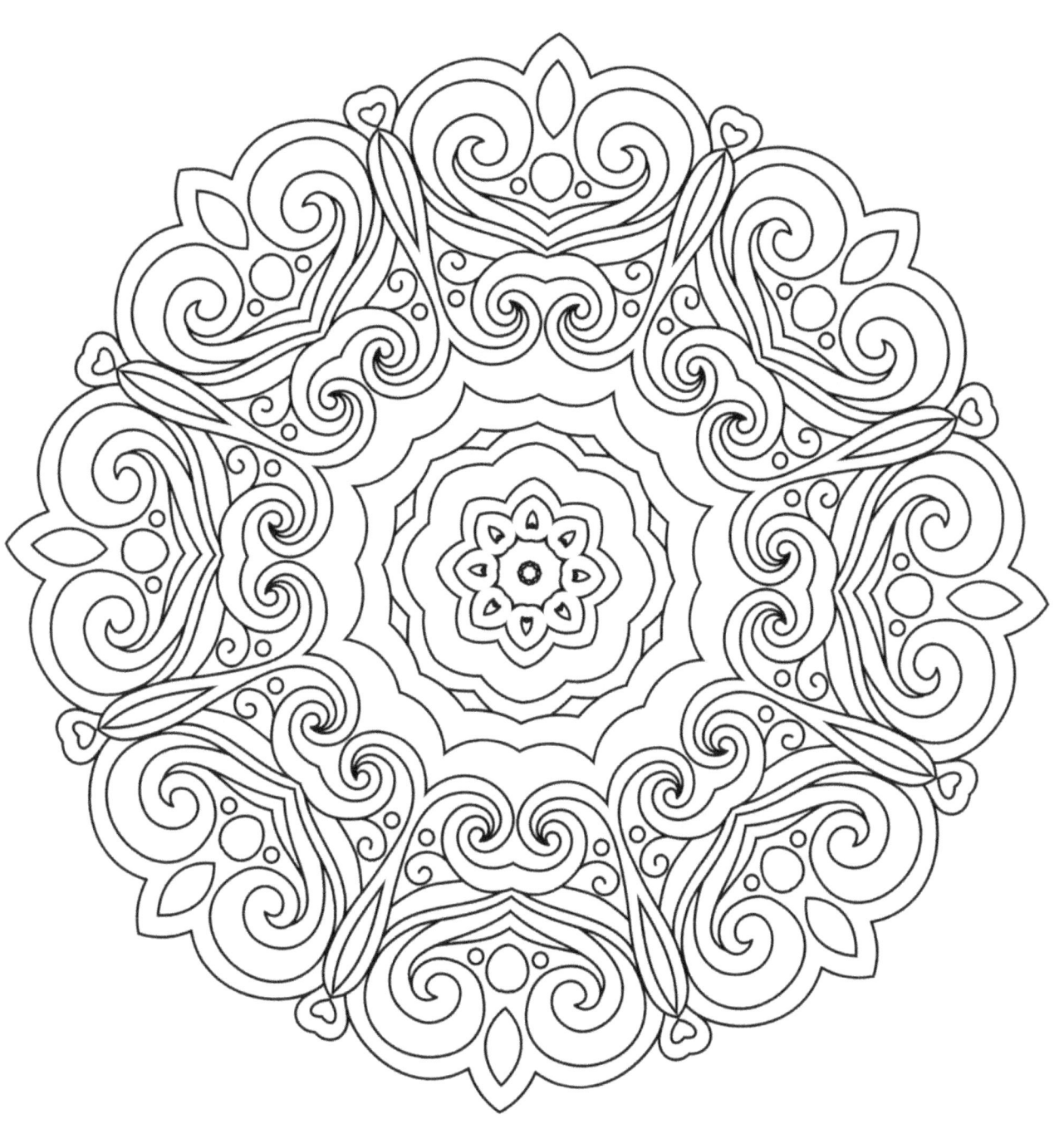

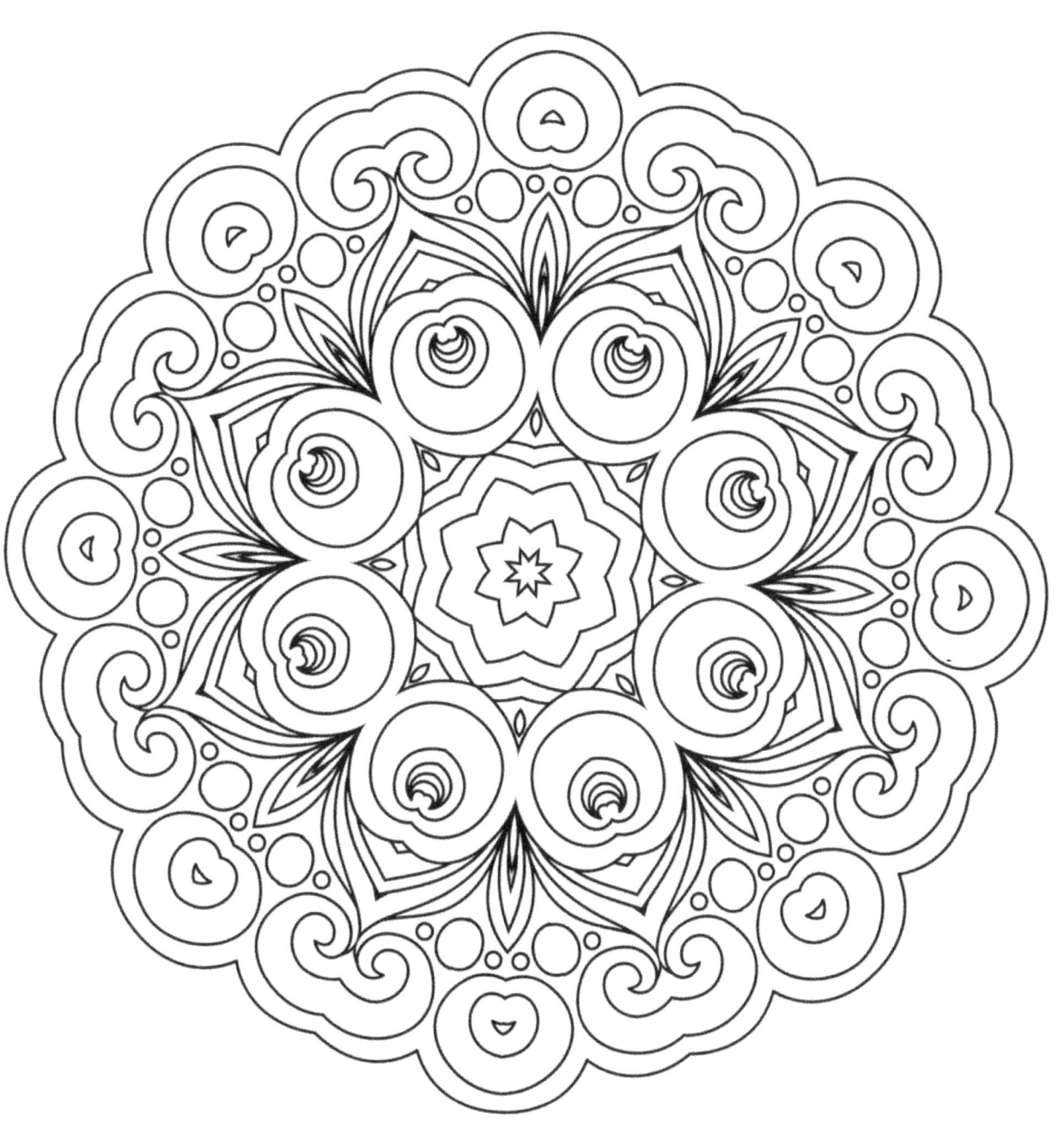

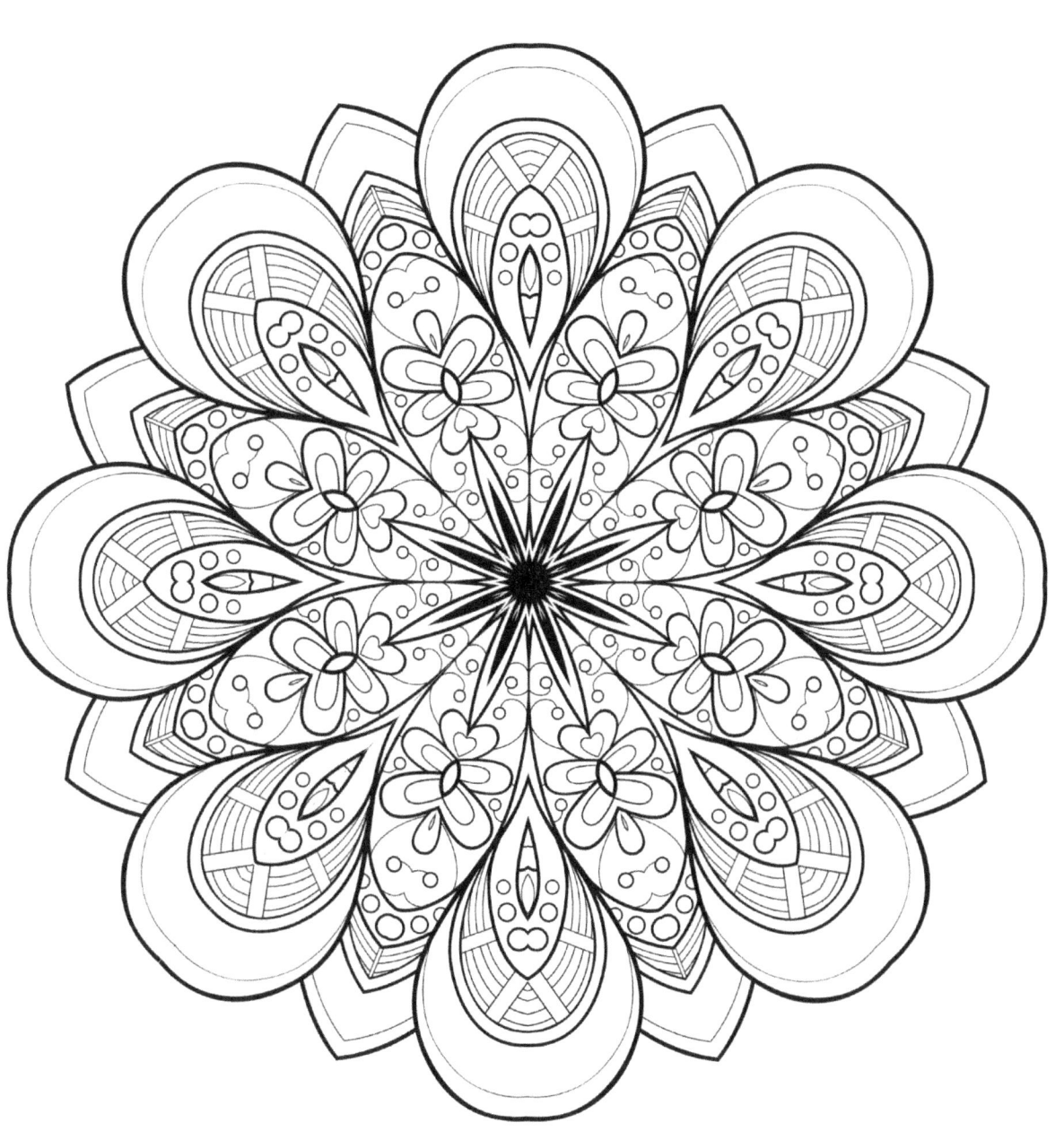

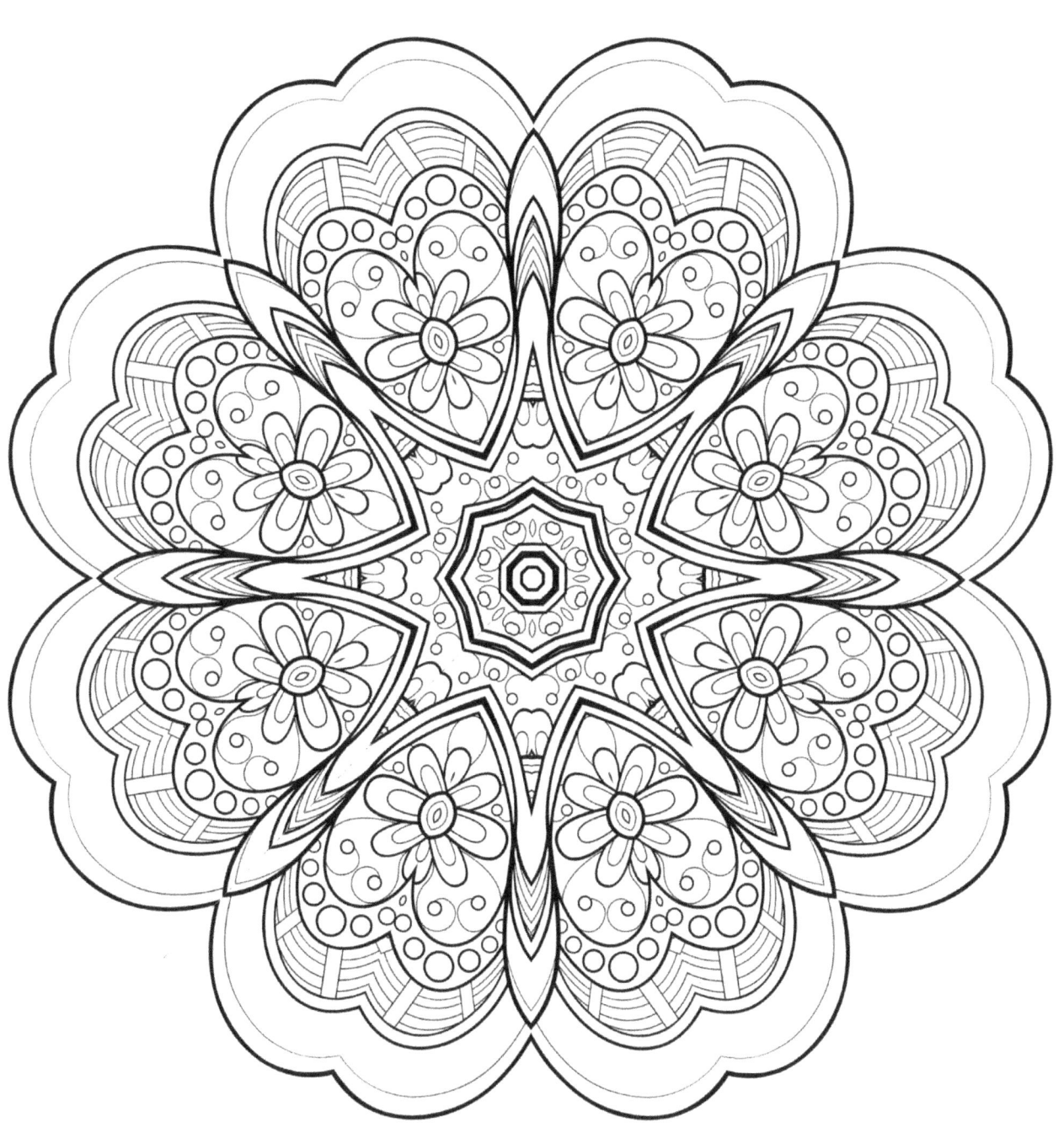

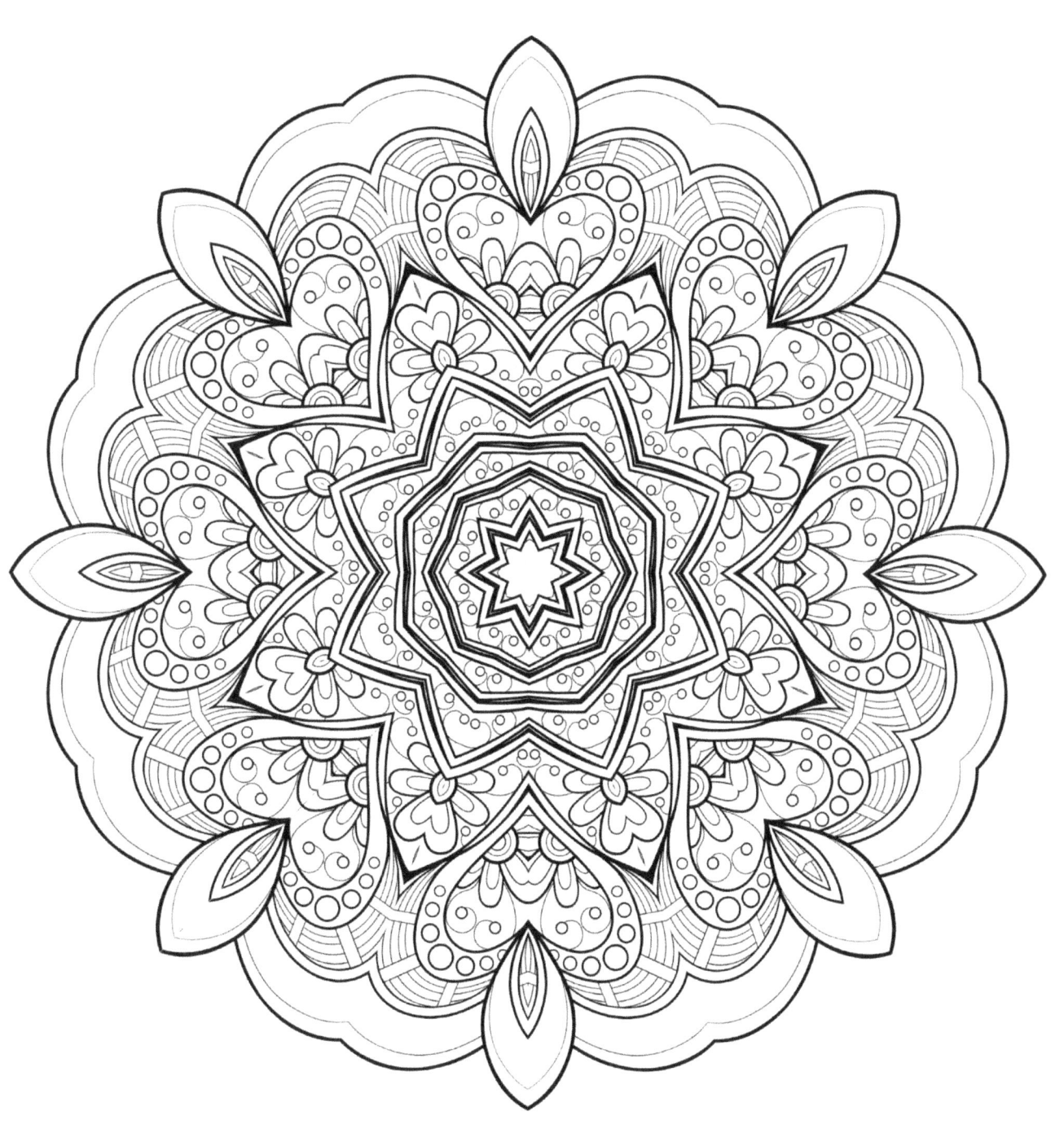

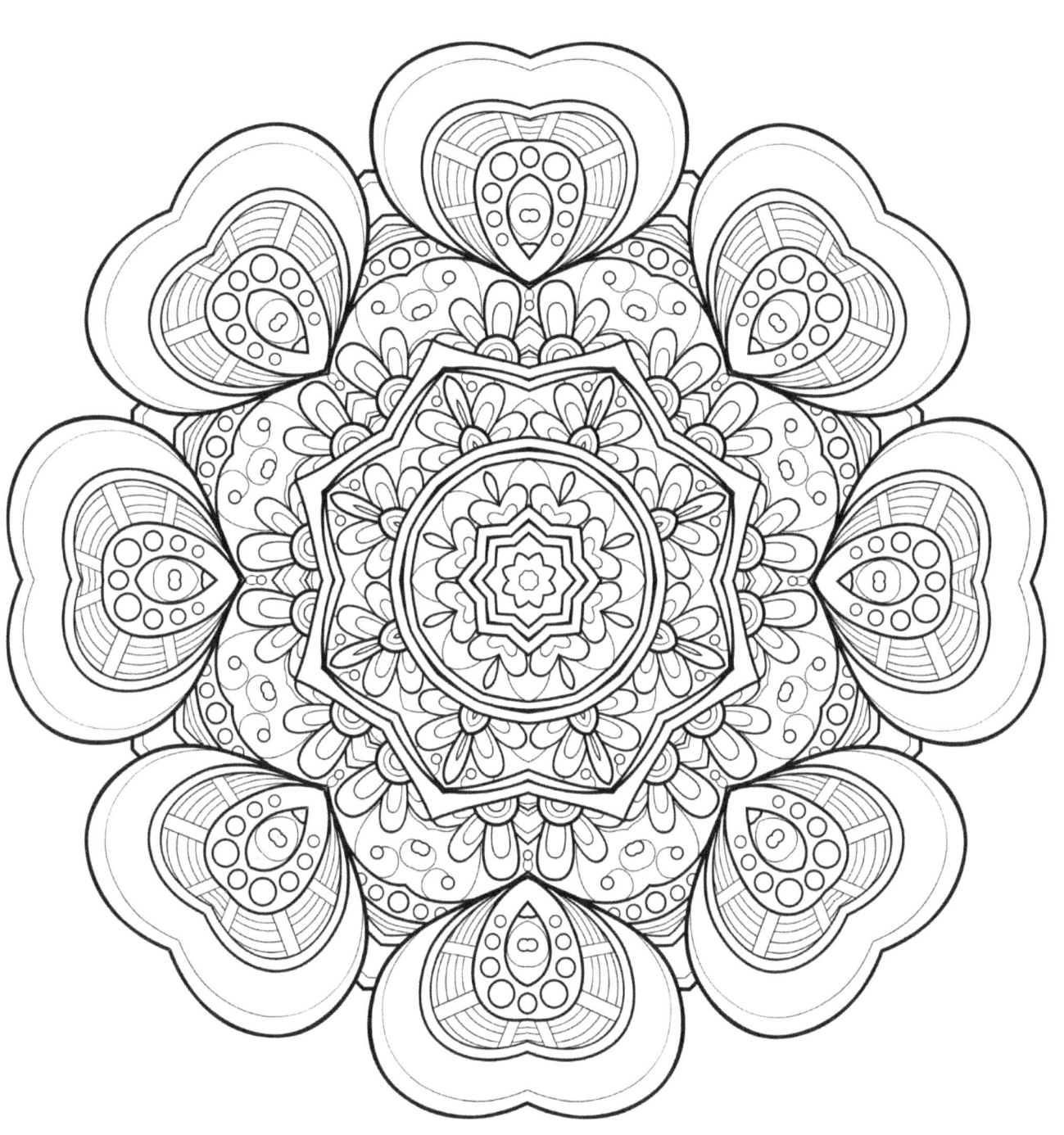

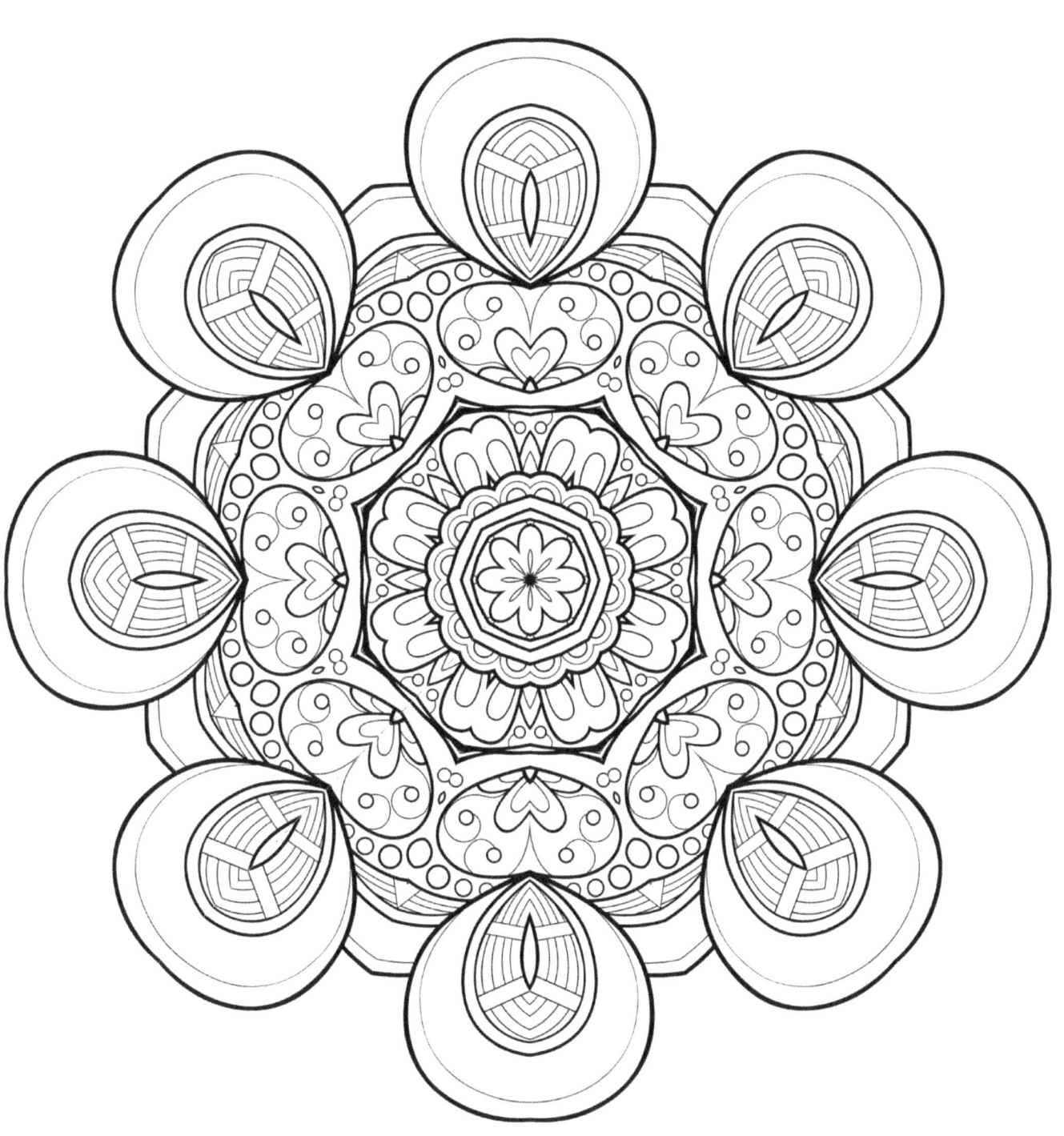

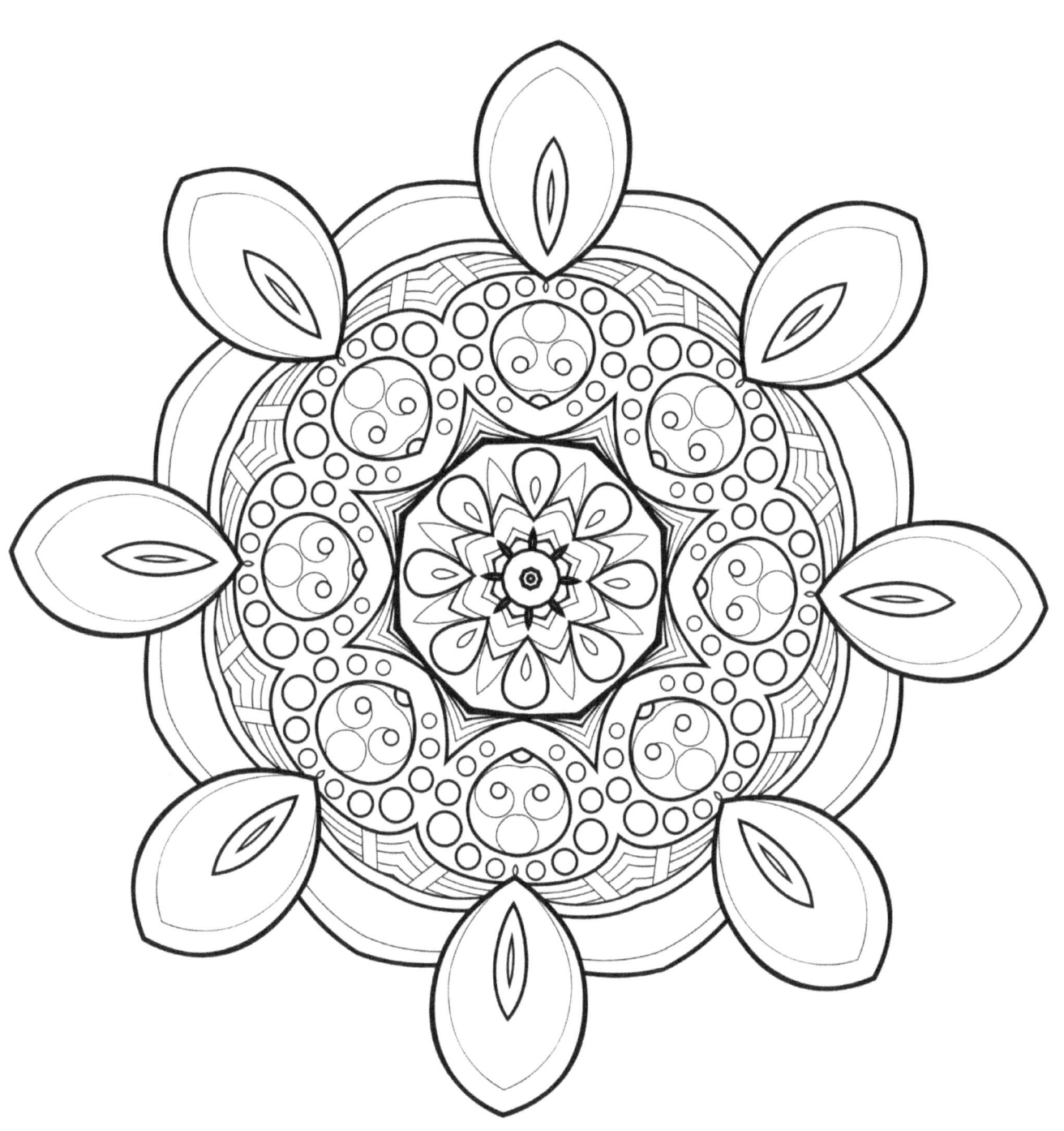

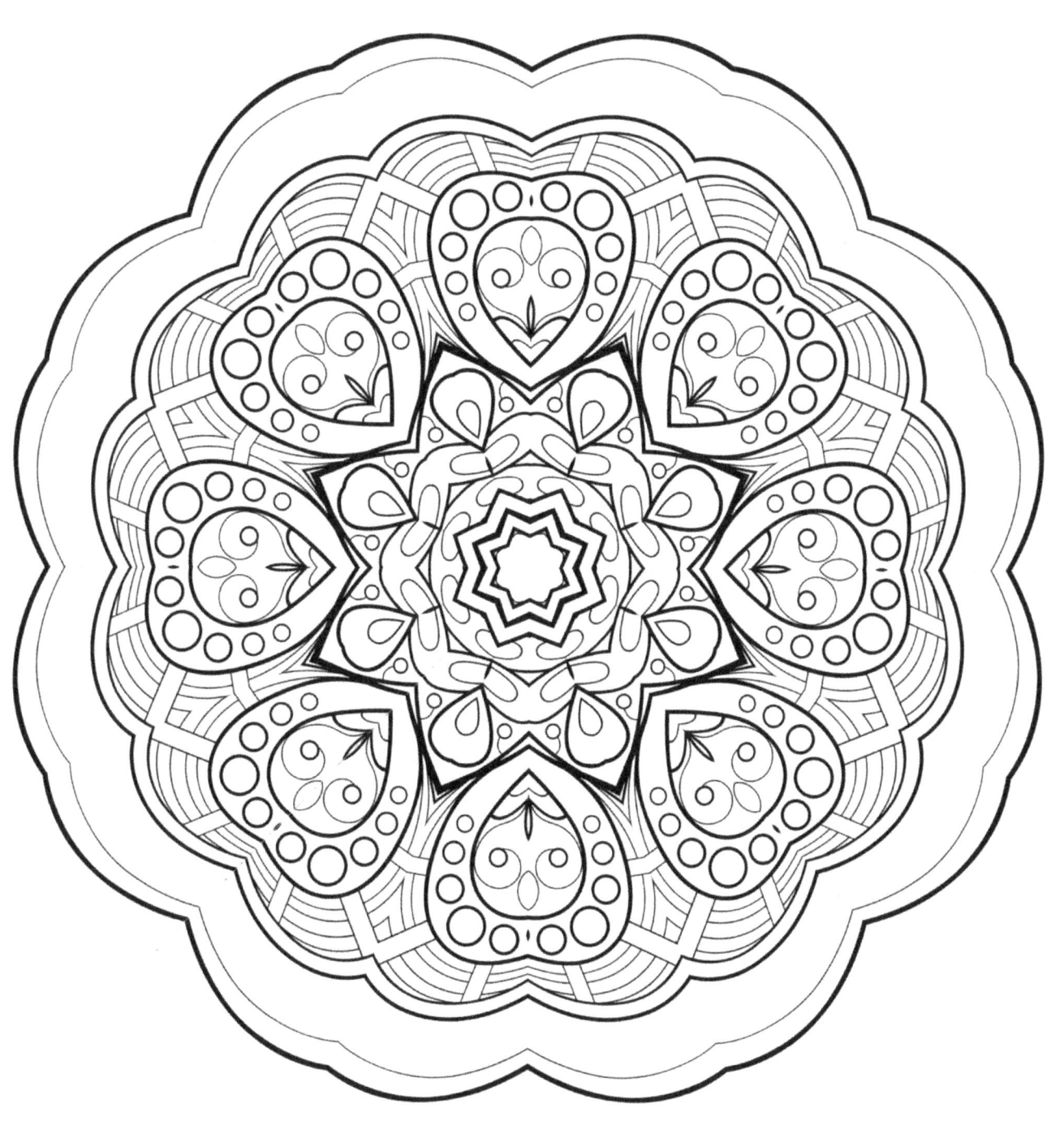

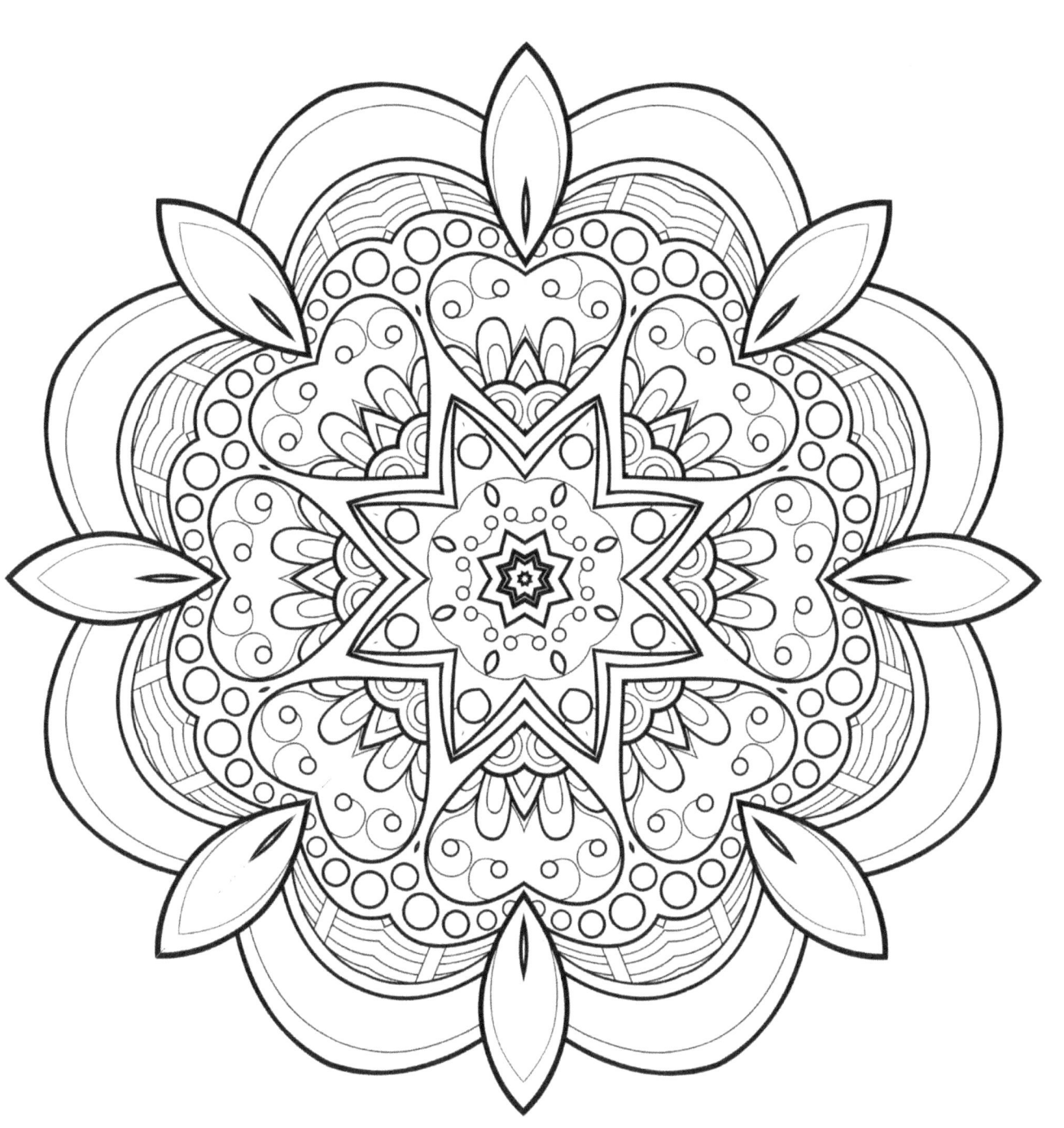

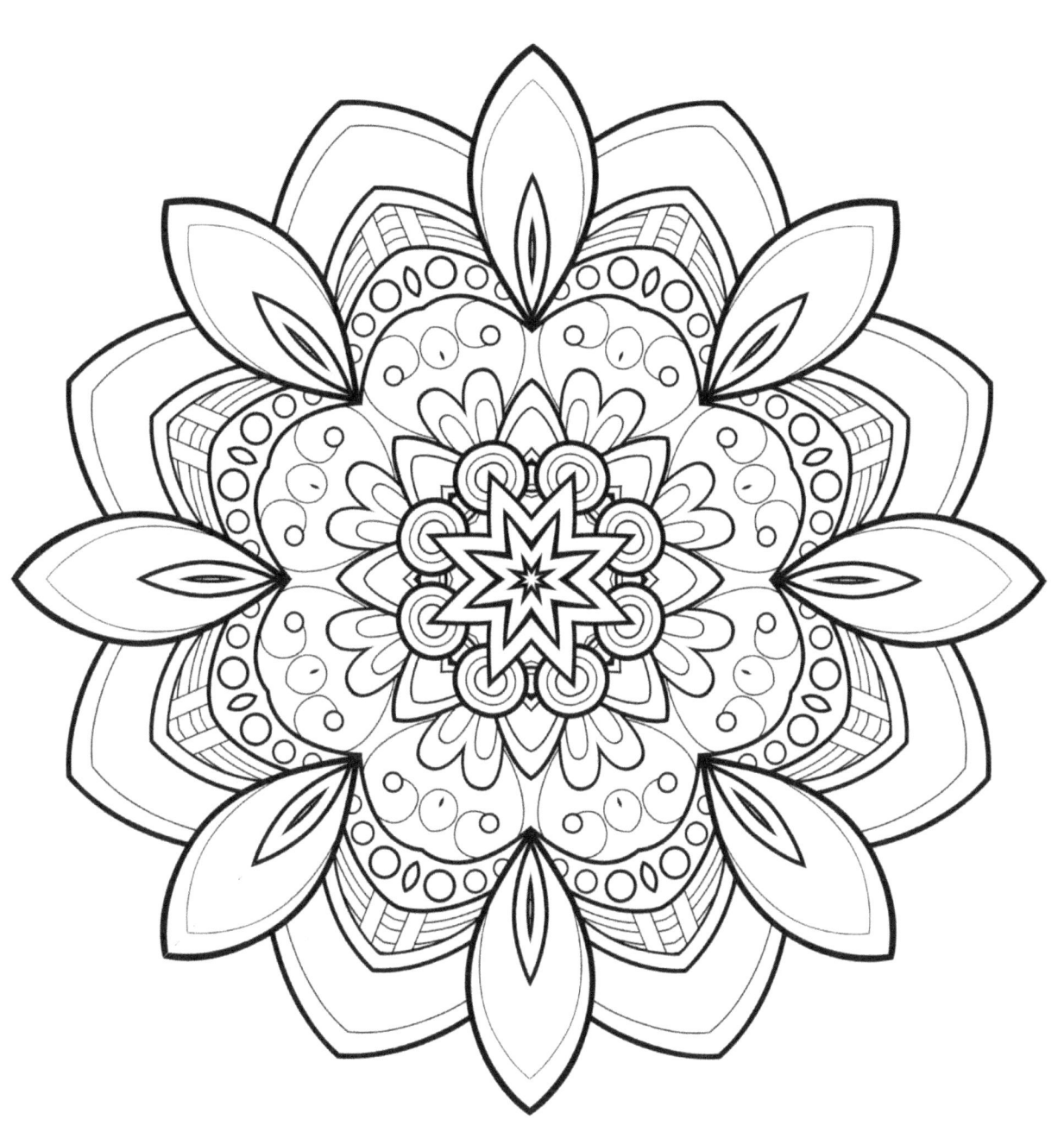

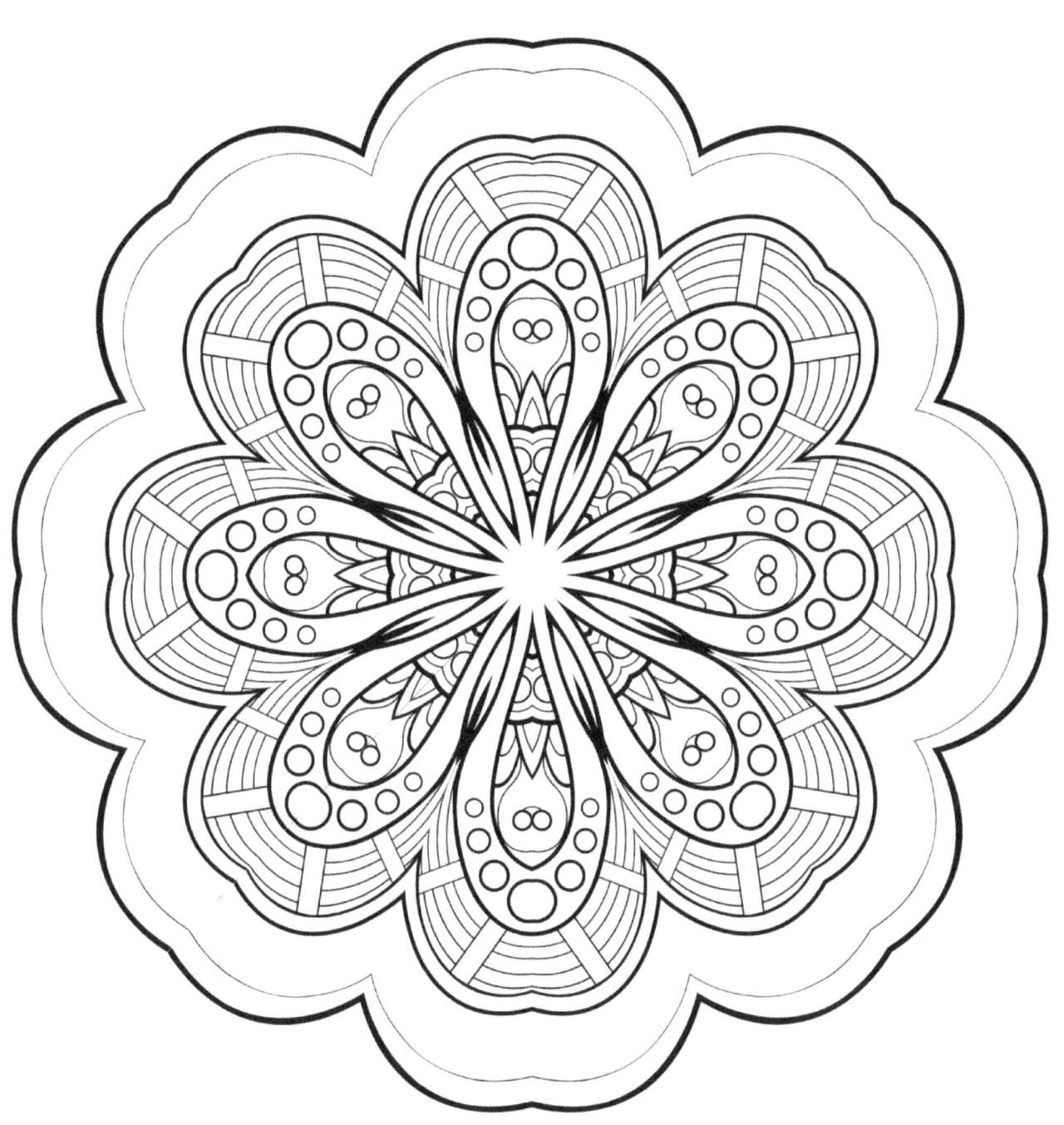

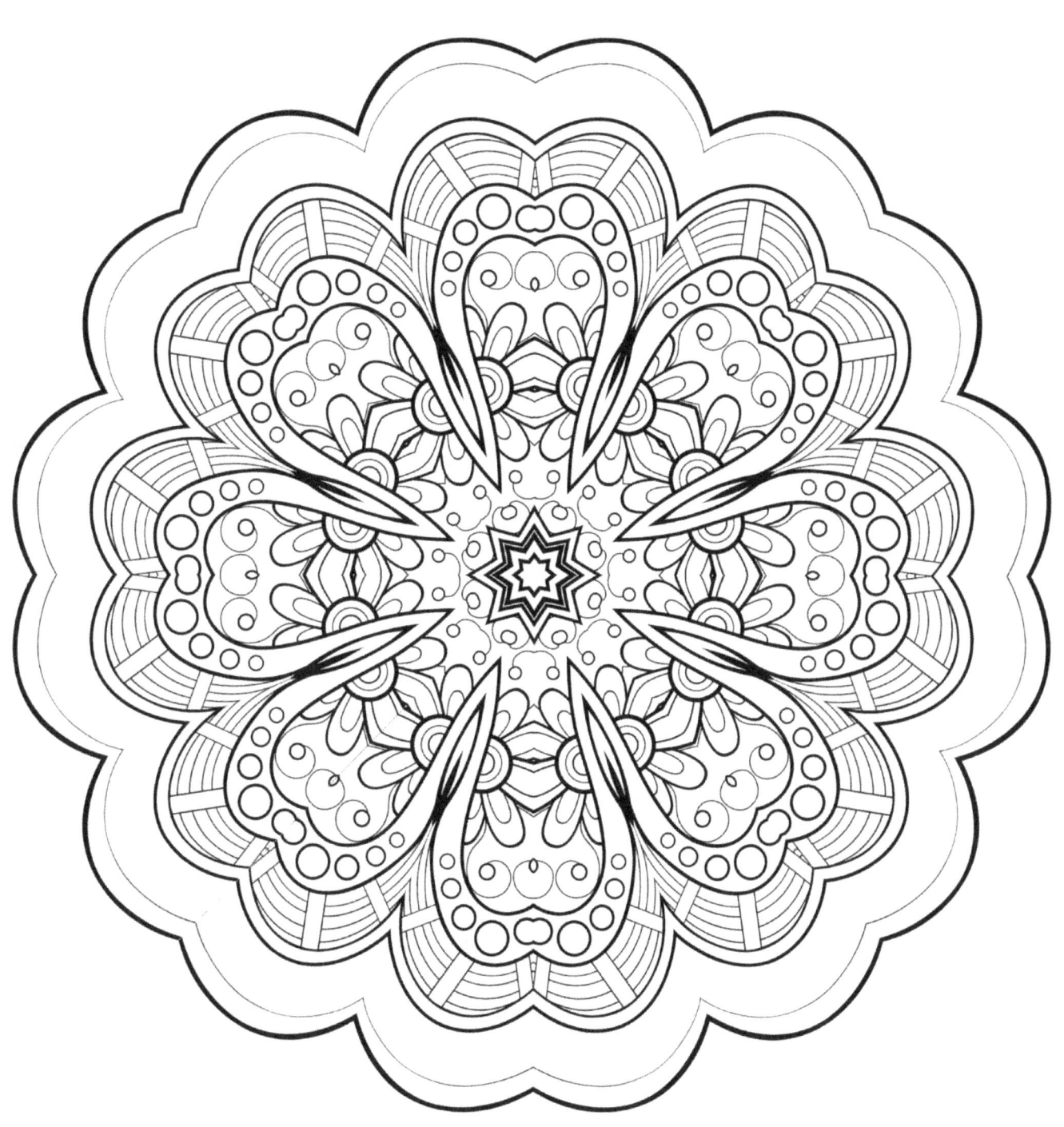

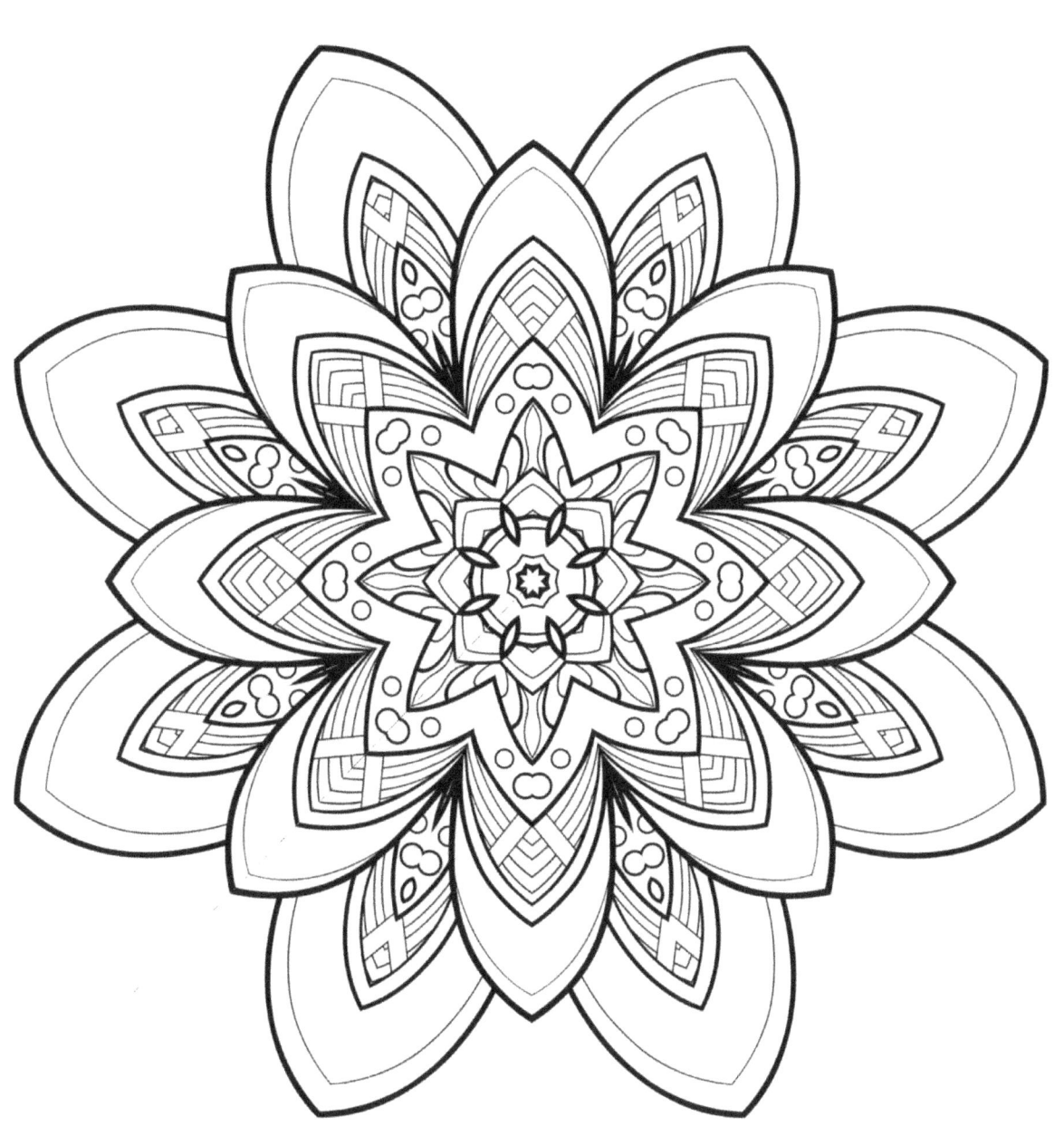

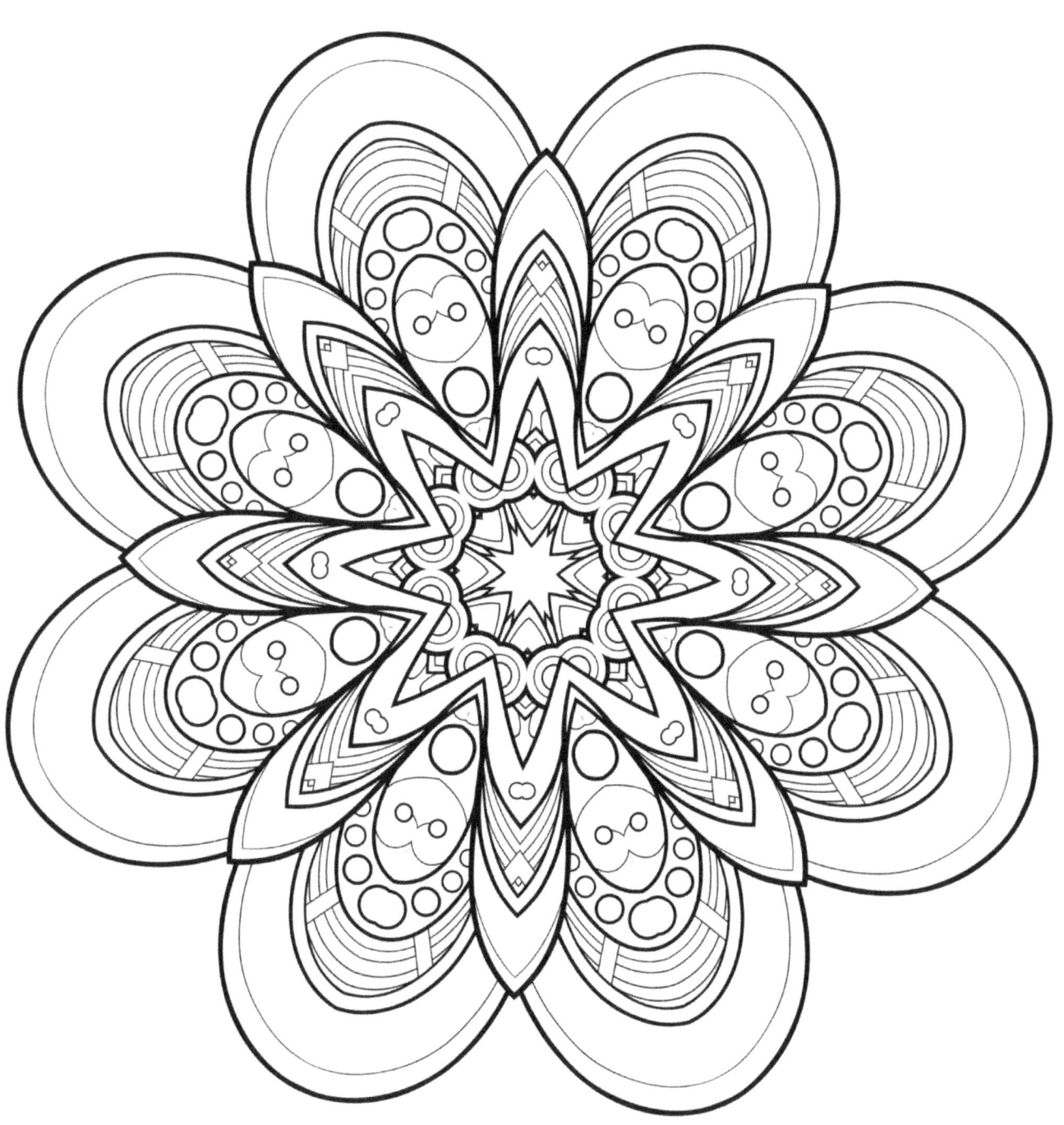

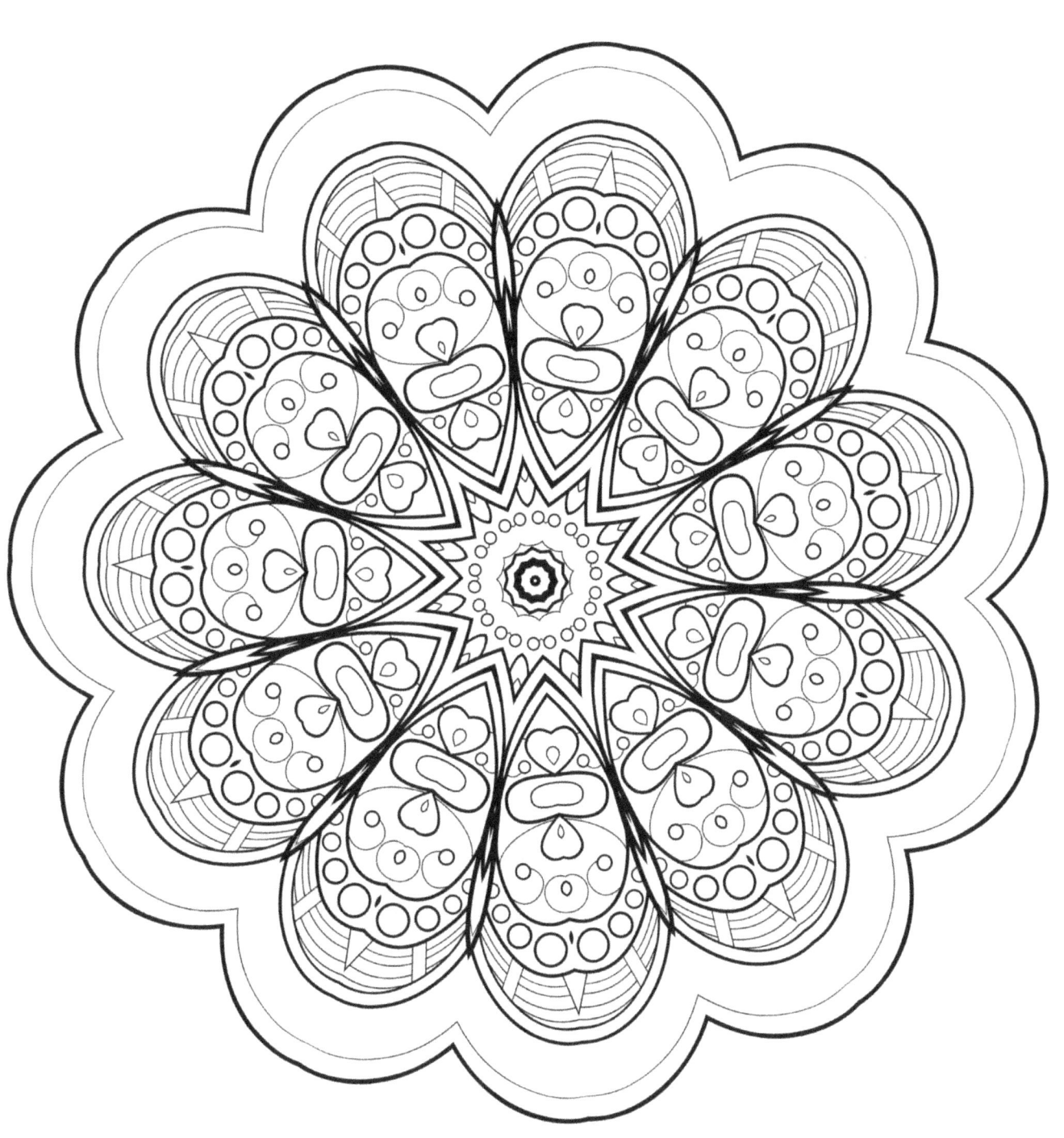

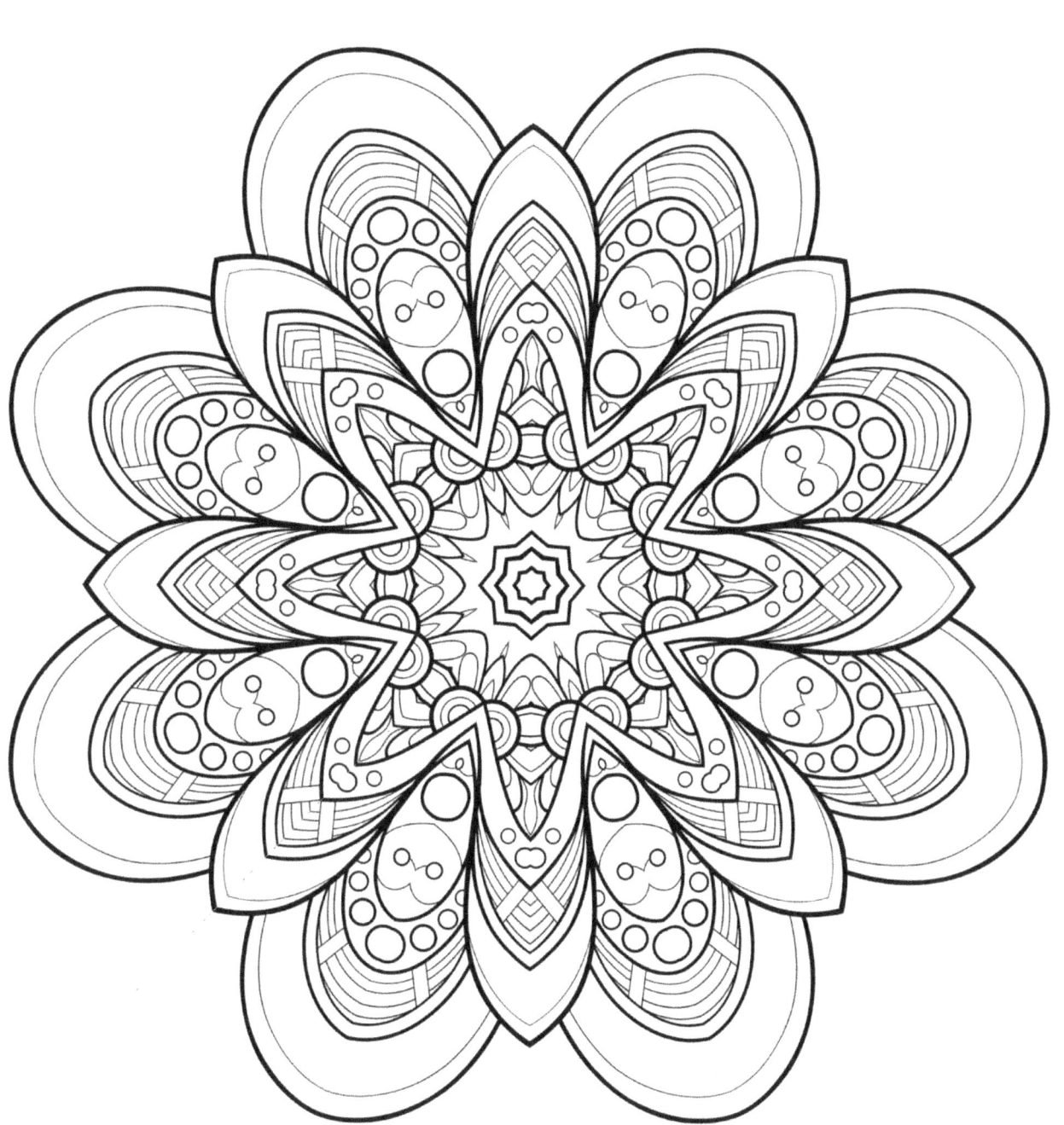

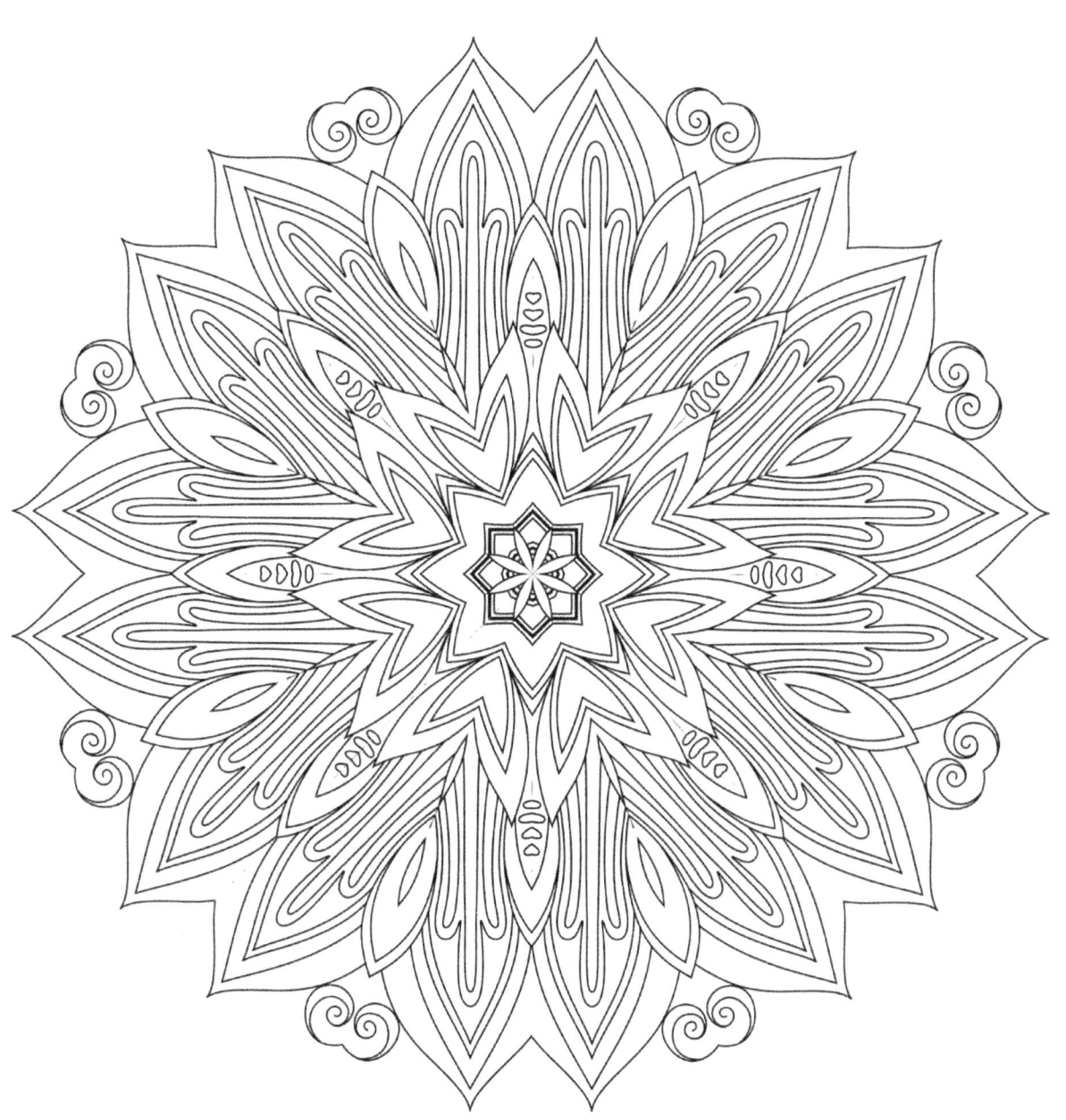

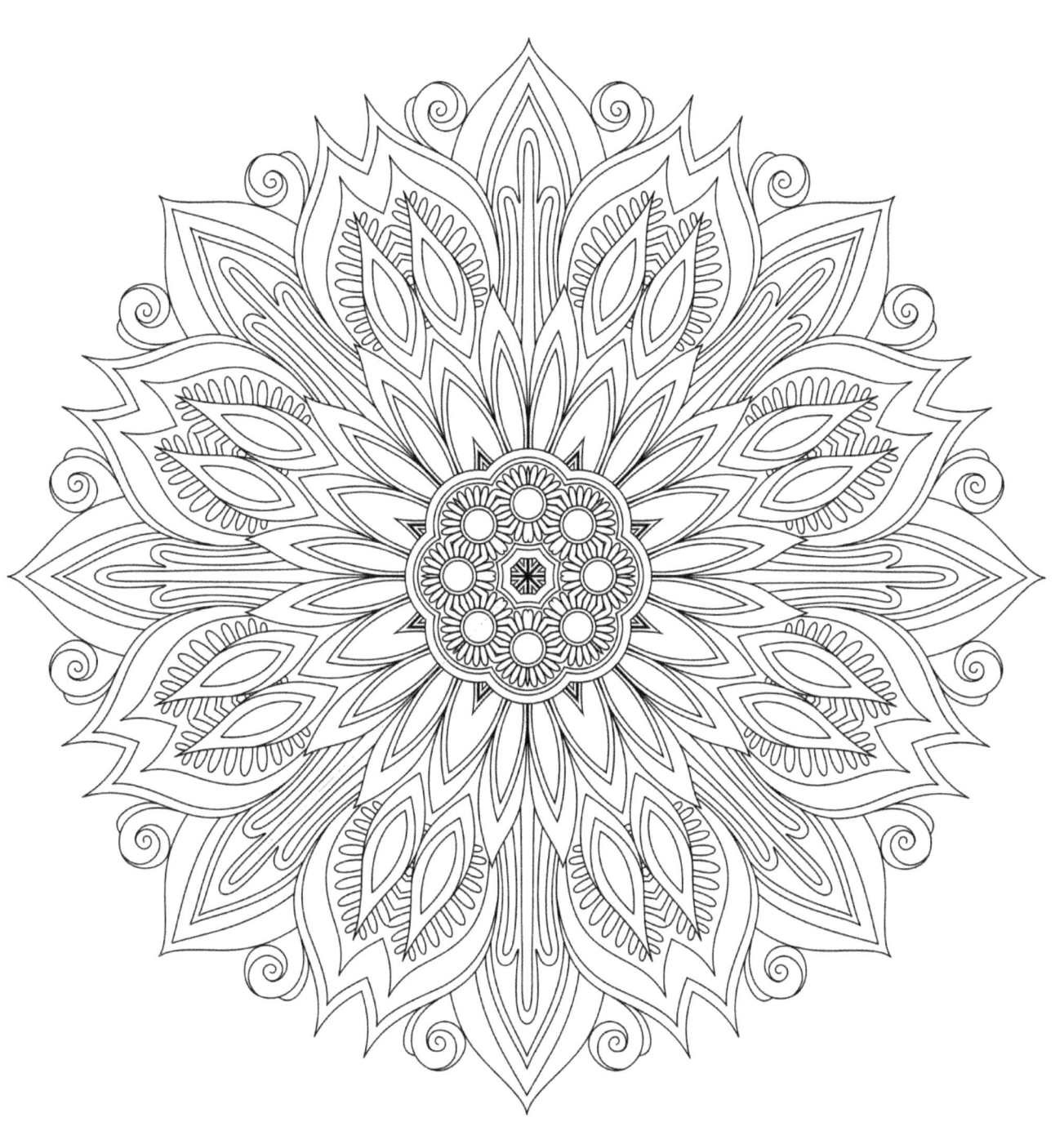

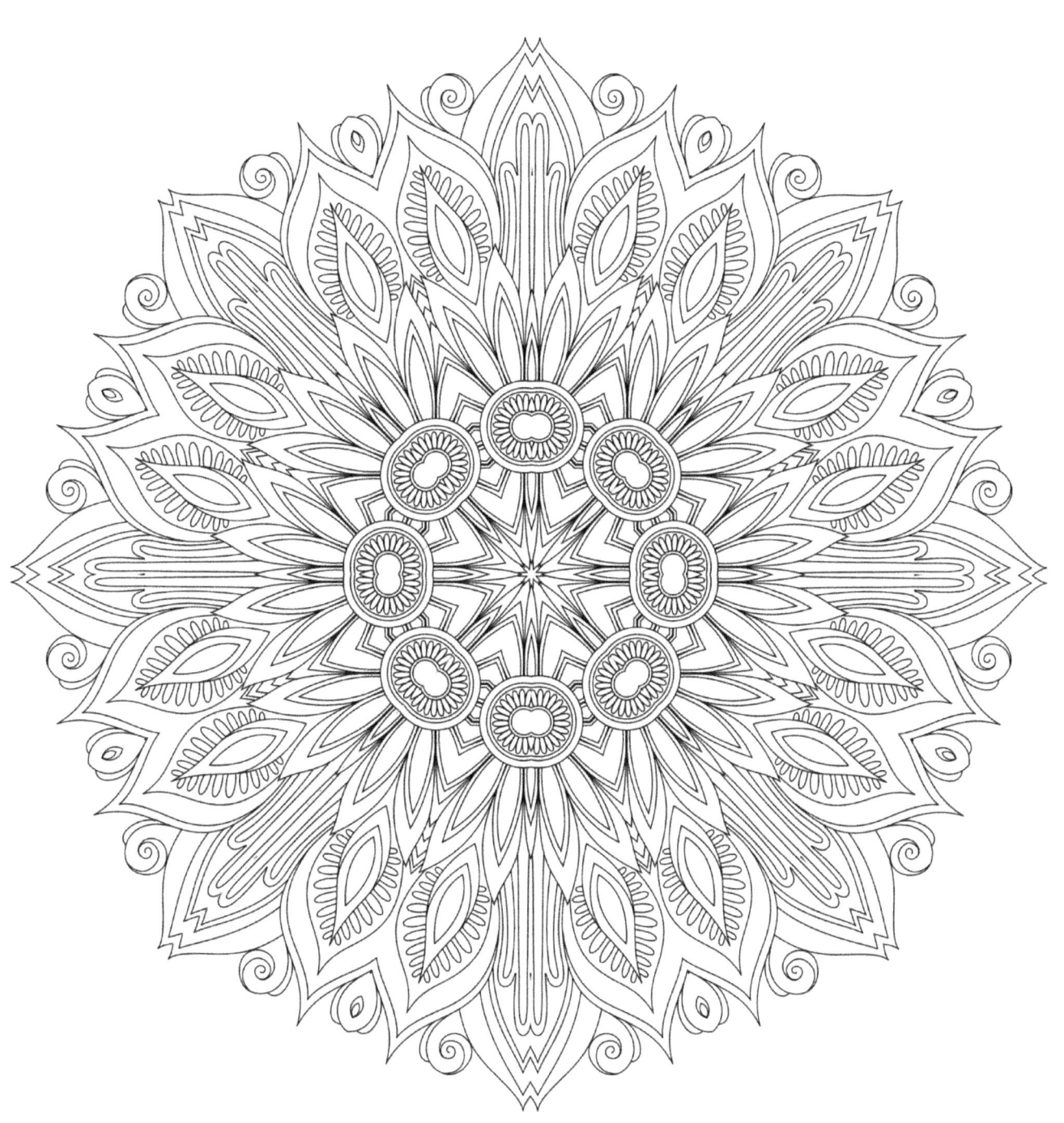

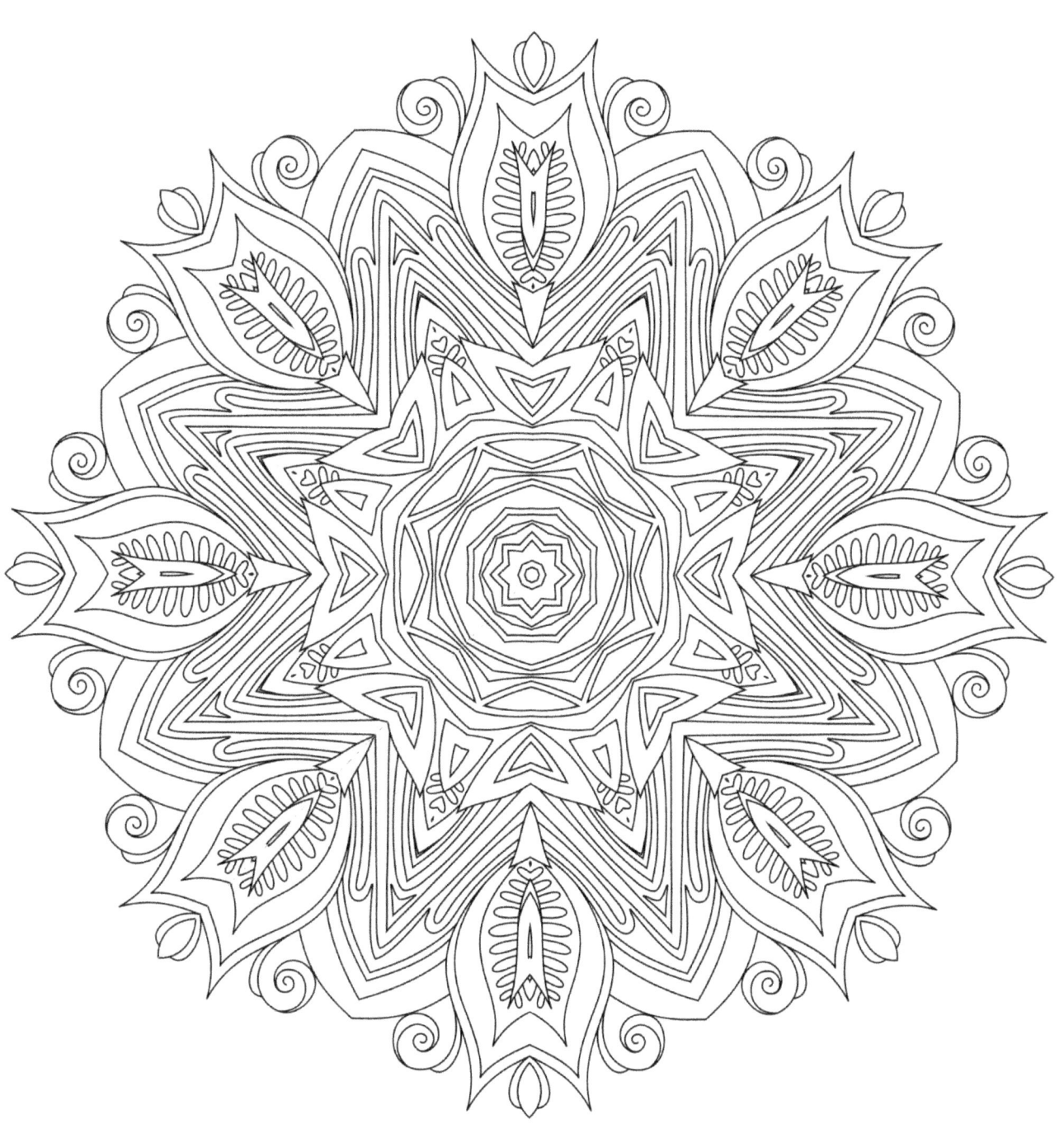

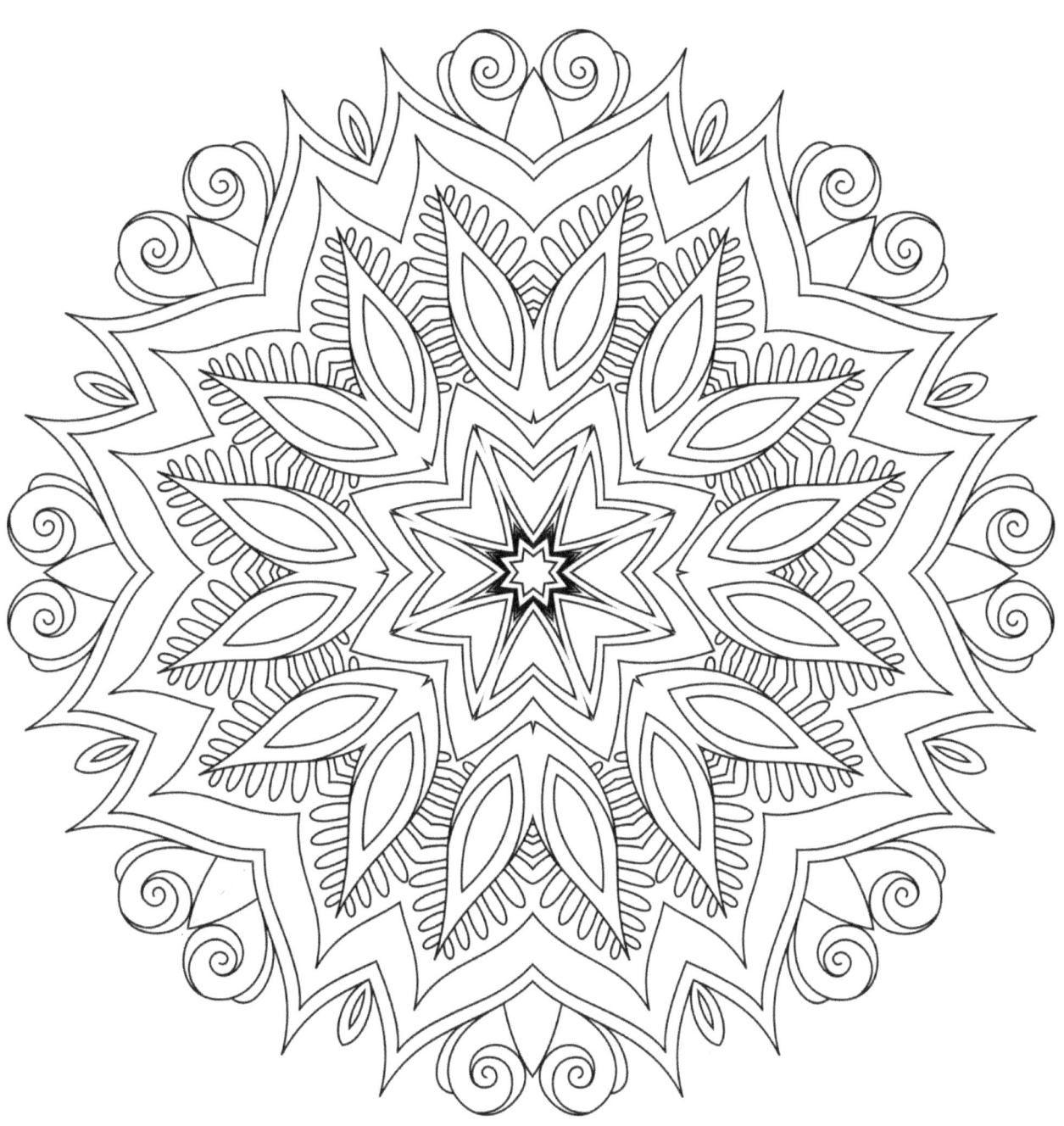

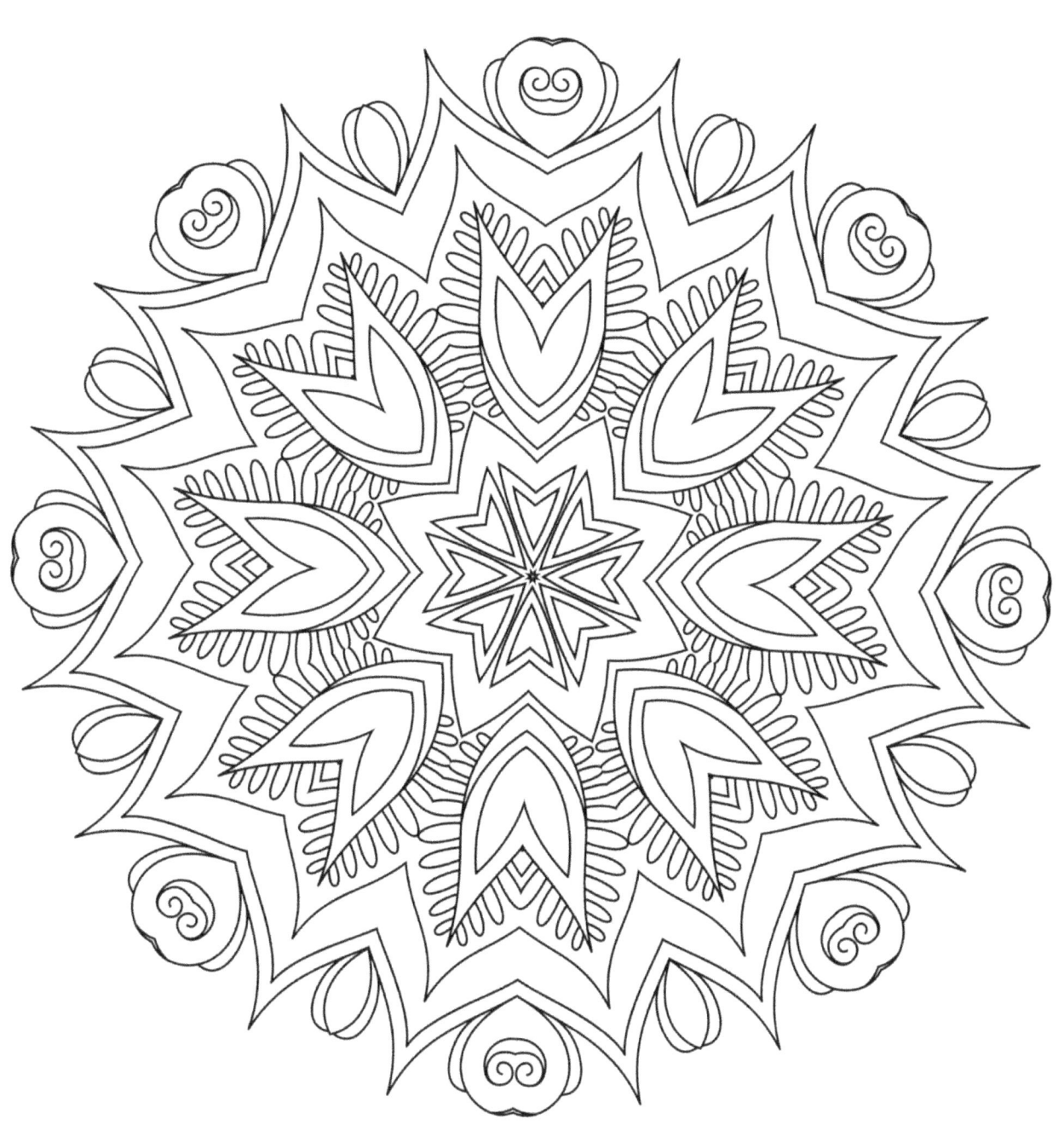

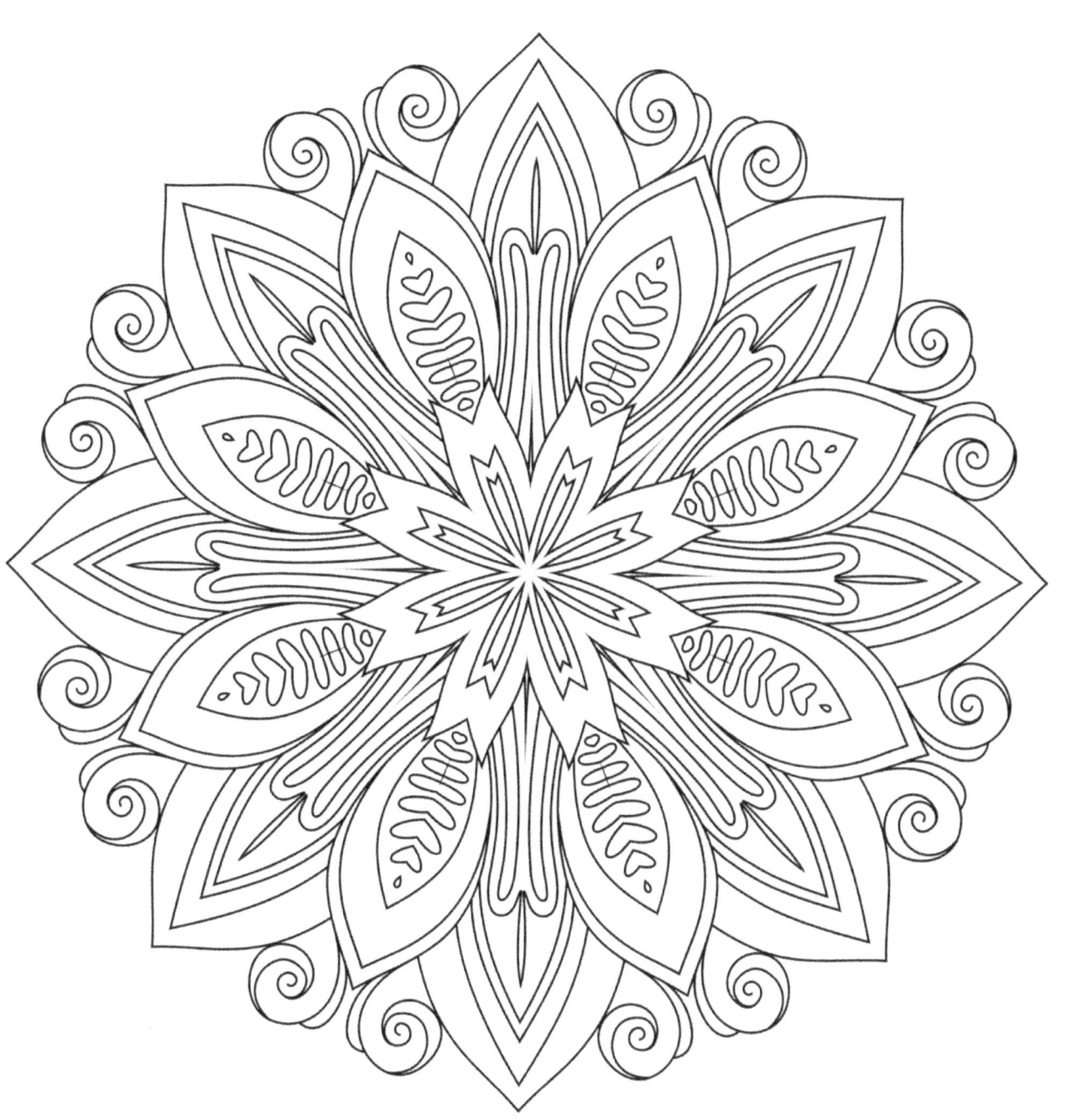

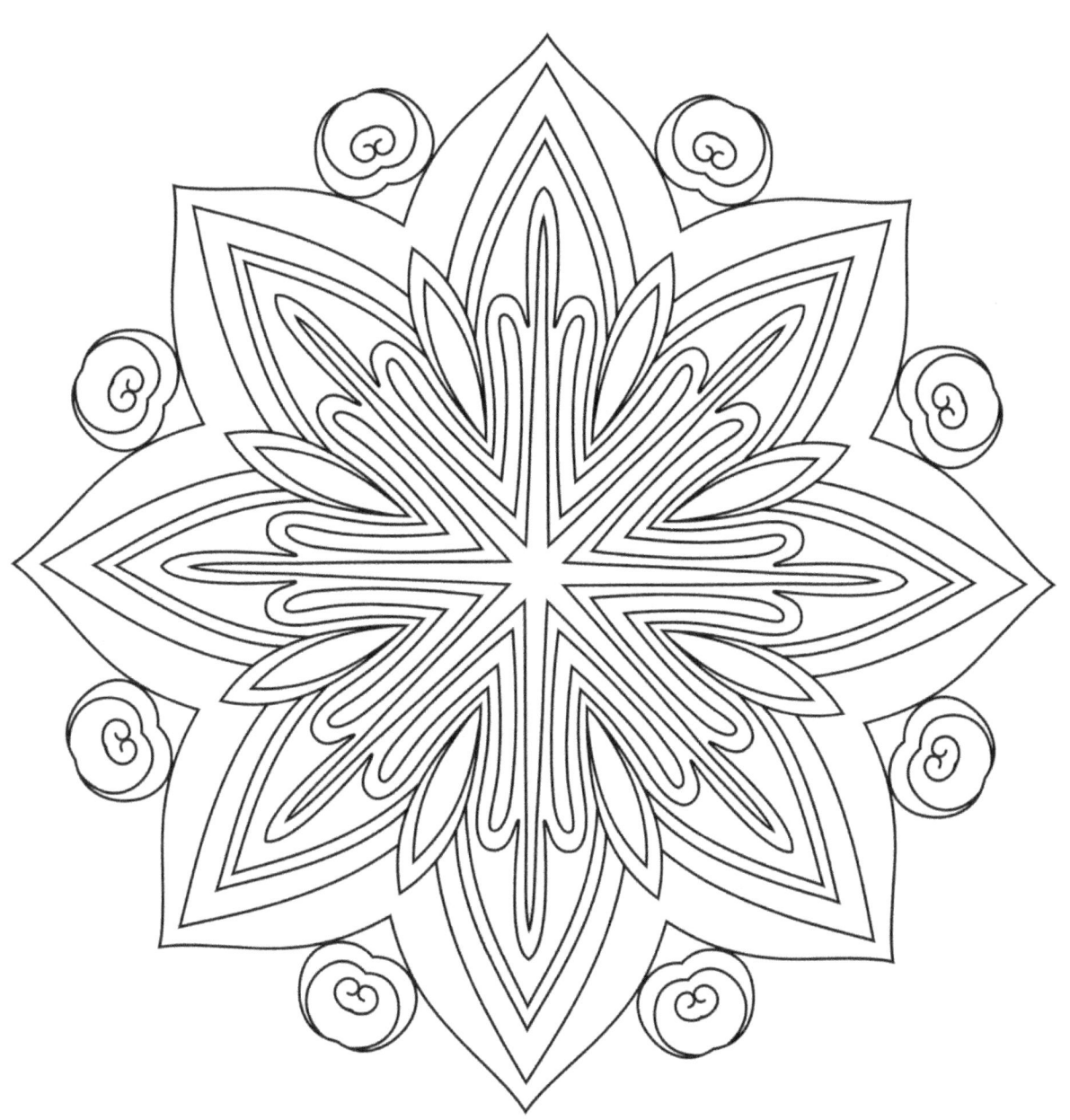

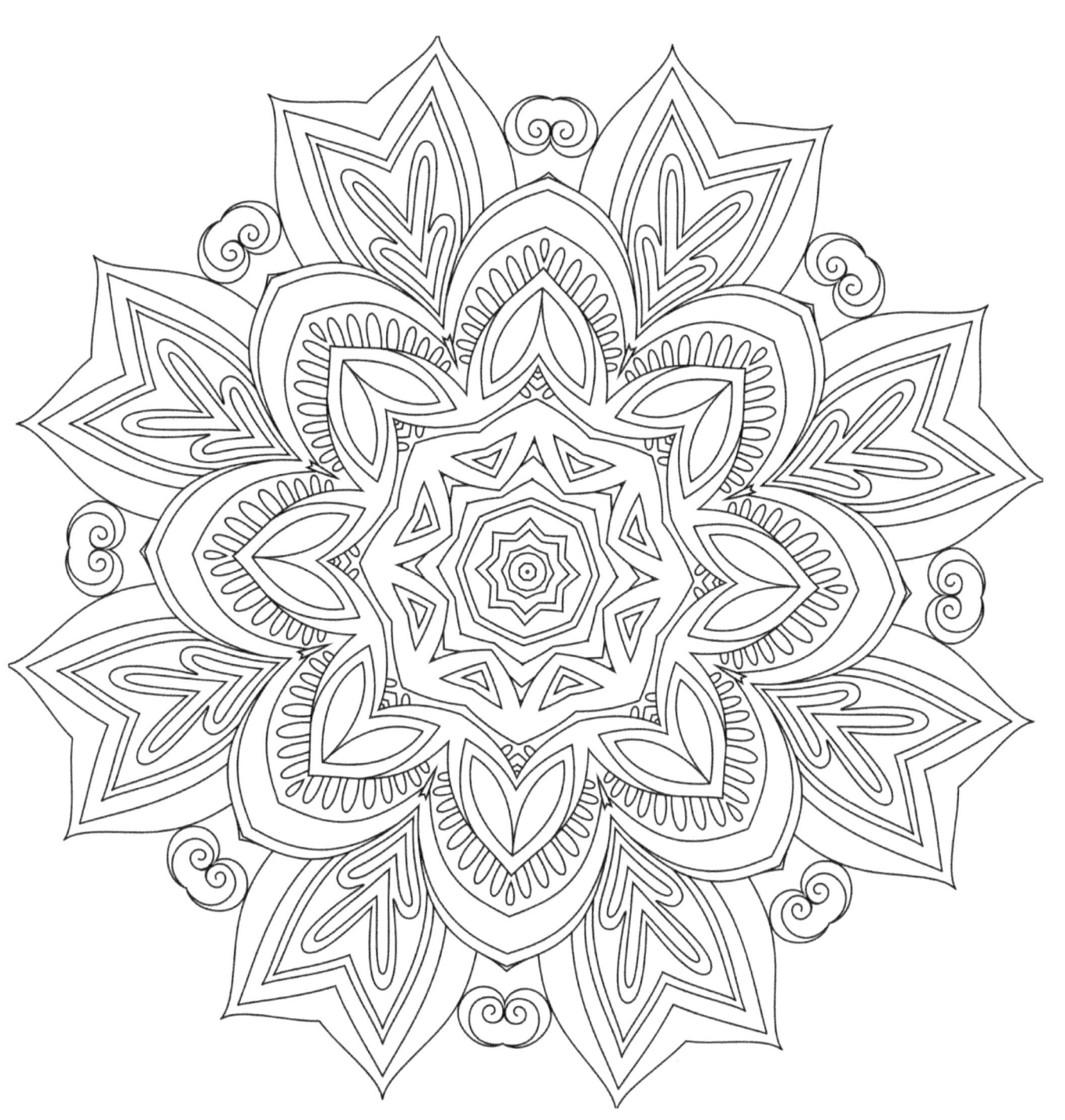

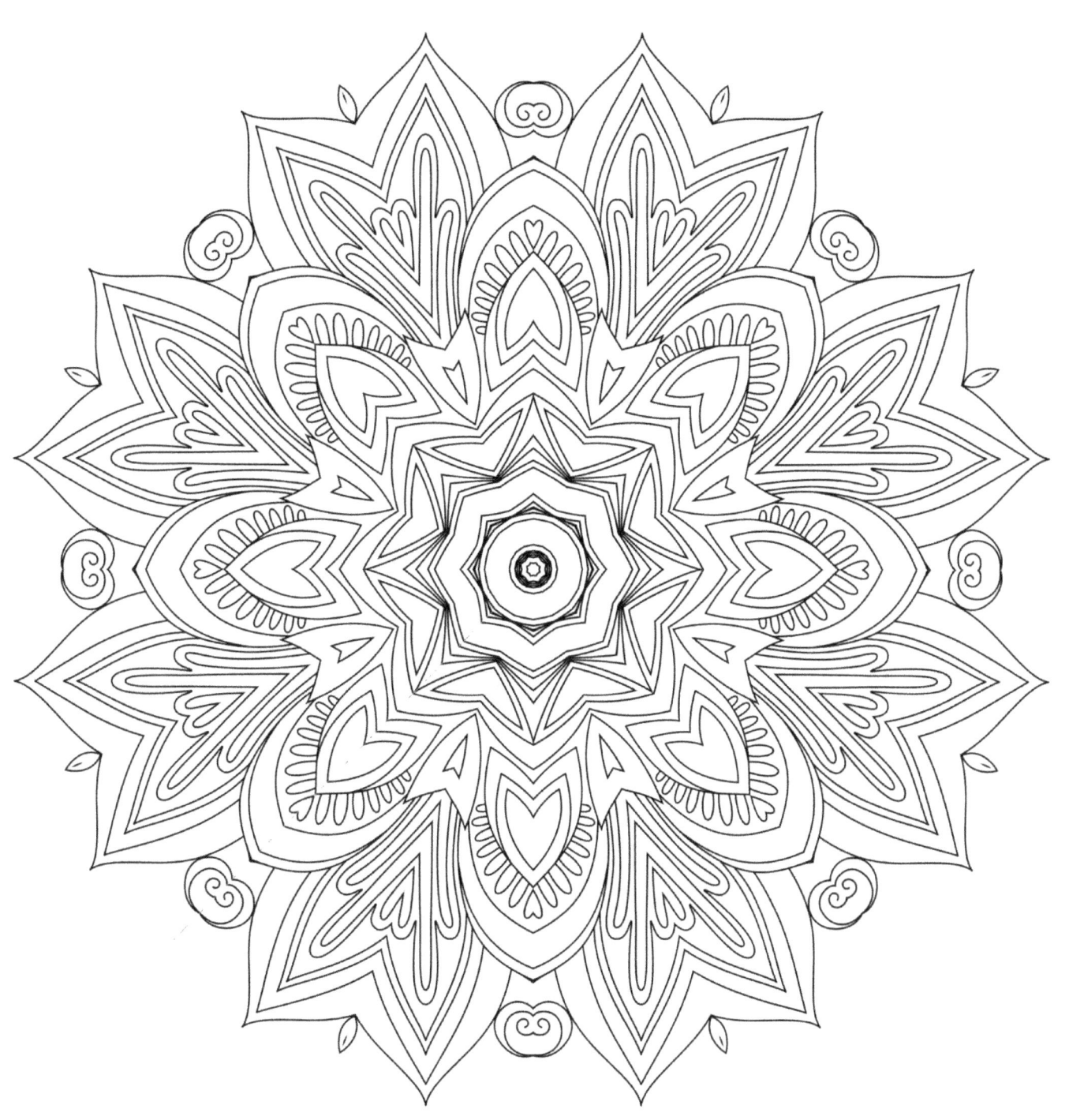

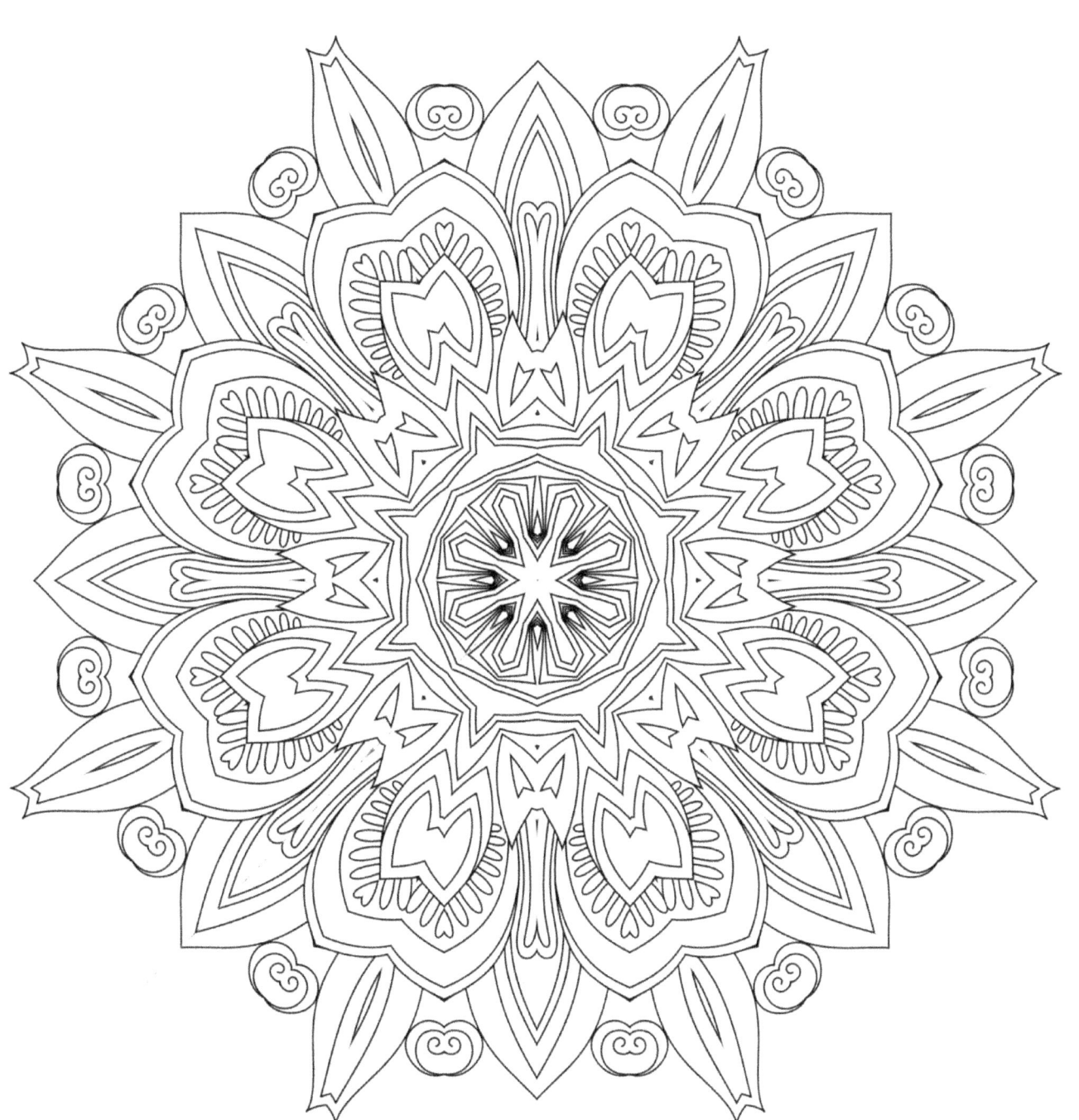

Hope you enjoy this coloring book.

Thank you.

www.ingramcontent.com/pod-product-compliance
Lightning Source LLC
Chambersburg PA
CBHW080836180526

45168CB00006B/2699